WHAT NEXT?

The Impact of AI on Modern Software

DAVE MULDOON

Book design by Launch My Book, Inc (www.launchmybook.com)
with cover design by Erika Alyana Duran (easduran.myportfolio.com)
and interior design by DTPerfect Book Design.

Published in the United States of America by Scale Up Technologies Ltd

Identifiers:
978-1-0687006-0-6 (Paperback)
978-1-0687006-1-3 (Ebook)

Dedication

To my wife Sorcha, my children Brídín, Aodán and Gráinne, my Mum, Dad, sisters and my extended family who put up with me, humor me (sometimes) and inspire me in ways they don't even know. Thanks guys, you are everything.

To colleagues I have worked with, done business with and learned from, far too many to name, thank you for the time we shared on the journey so far.

Oh, and reach out and talk to a friend today. You never know what they might be going through.

Contents

Introduction

Welcome to the new era. An era where the world of software is being ripped open and massively disrupted. Between 2024 and 2027, every aspect of modern software—how it is dreamed up, defined, designed, written, tested, refined, deployed and used—will be completely changed. New artificial intelligence capabilities powered by the economics and architecture of the cloud will mean that a large part of what we know today as software will disappear, be displaced or evolve significantly. A lot of change is going to happen rapidly, taking some of us by complete surprise. Companies will find their software stack obsolete or outdated. Many applications will lack new features offered by disruptive emerging startups.

As we trace the history of artificial intelligence (AI) to place the recent changes in context, we will see the technology evolving from ideas that were first written about in the 1940s and '50s. During previous waves of change, I observed that once the initial hype fades, people go back to working, looking after family, being with friends and spending time on hobbies. For this reason, I wrote this book as a call to action. The impact of AI could be very swift and quite messy for anyone who is ill-prepared.

When ChatGPT was released in November 2022, it signaled the first emergence of AI into mainstream society. A few things have since become clear:

- The way we design and build software will change utterly.

- The software we create will be very different.

- The way we use software will shift dramatically.

I will examine these points in the chapters that follow and attempt to explore the impact AI will have on our profession and industry. It is not obvious to state that AI is just software. All the components that are used to create AI solutions are made from software. What we can see happening now is that these latest AI capabilities are shaking up an entire software ecosystem that has grown organically for a few decades now. We will trace the development of some of the technologies and aspects that have led to AI becoming a disruptive force in modern software. Briefly, here are some of the main reasons behind the recent explosion:

- The development of new models / architectures that allow software to learn faster and be more affordable.

- The sheer amount of data that can be generated and analyzed at scale is mind-blowing.

- Faster compute power made possible by newer chipsets and cloud platforms have led to a dramatic increase in affordable computing power.

- Everyone from researchers to large companies are making their code and ideas available as open source, which has accelerated the pace of progress.

By examining how AI has emerged, I am really hoping that it influences the reader to take it seriously. Many of us will become bored of seeing AI tagged into every new technology product that is launched. I am urging you to see through the hype and engage in some critical analysis. People in the business of software and technology should especially start thinking about all the ways that AI will influence the industry they work in, the company they work with and the role they perform. Everyone involved in designing, developing, testing, supporting, selling and writing about software can use this book as a starting point.

In certain sections I'm taking a guess on what the future holds. Some things are obvious, others you will likely disagree with. AI is about to mess with our concept of time because it will make technology change more rapid. The point is, I want you to think about your role today and what your role will look like in 2027 and start to equip yourself for the journey ahead. I want you to thrive, and as Darwin put it, be "the one that is most adaptable to change."

I think it's important to note how I used AI in the research and writing of this book. Throughout January and Februaury 2024, I used a combination of Google Search, ChatGPT and Google Bard (as it was known then) to help carry out the main research into the key concepts for the book. I used ChatGPT to create the response noted in the book, and Google Gemini (as it was later rebranded) to create the alternative ending.

ChatGPT and Gemini advanced edition were also used extensively to summarise research papers and web-based material to help review their relevance. This helped me cut through a lot of papers that were less topical and therefore not referenced. All other content was written by the author.

All the diagrams were created by the author in PowerPoint and I used paid-for stock images sourced from Dreamstime.com. Finally, I partnered with the team at launchmybook.com for professional copy editing, book cover design, interior design and ebook preparation.

A Brief History of Change

"AI is likely to be either the best or worst thing to happen to humanity."

—STEPHEN HAWKING

I am fascinated by change, having worked for more than thirty years in a variety of roles, in different industries and businesses, always with a technology focus. I've seen and been a part of so many waves of change. While I was in college, the internet first emerged, and we saw the first Mosaic browser on basic 486 PCs with limited graphics. I started my career programming a mainframe in a bank, but I quickly wanted to get involved in internet technologies that I suspected would disrupt the world of software. As it turned out, the web had a profound impact, and I eventually started and sold a business that customized these web-based software platforms.

I can still recall the excitement when the first PC came into our house. Sometime in late 1984 or early '85, my dad worked for the national electricity utility in Ireland and they were helping staff to purchase a home computer. They were not cheap back then, so he had to spread out the monthly payments over multiple years. It was an Amstrad CPC 6128 with a green screen, floppy disk drive and 128k of RAM. I distinctly remember that it came bundled with DR Logo's turtle graphics. On the back cover of the instruction book, it promised, "Designed with the user in mind, Logo builds programs from simple English-like commands that are immediately understandable."

Loading this program from a floppy disk, you were presented with a prompt. I can still picture this basic green screen with its terrible fonts.

```
LOGO Turtle-Graphics Interpreter
© S.J.Wainwright.1984.
Input resolution m or l  ? ■
```

FIGURE 1. *Turtle graphics 1984.*

Giving a series of commands and instructions, you could move the cursor, a little turtle, around the screen and get it to paint shapes and lines in whatever color (or shade of green) that you wished. This was our idea of fun back then! It's only now that I notice the question mark at the end. The machine is patiently prompting for input. Imagine for a second that we are back in 1984, before the internet, before the cloud and before the smartphone. Picture all of the life-changing developments in technology that have happened since then. Are we just past the turtle graphics stage of AI? Yes. Will such a massive set of changes happen again in the coming wave? The only answer I can offer is: yes, of course it will. AI is already bringing generational-defining disruptions across:

- the roles of software professionals (people)

- methods used to create and run software (process)

- the architecture and design of software (technology)

FIGURE 2. *Driving forces of change.*

We will also see change in all three layers at the same time, where completely new tools and features in one layer will affect and influence changes in the other two layers. This will have a compound effect, and these driving forces of change will seriously impact how we think and act in the software creation process.

Over the last eighty years, the world of technology has been evolving constantly in the pursuit of progress in almost every aspect of life. As humans, we have this innate drive within us to seek a better way, to take something that works and improve on it. Sometimes, the technology we create can be harmful to us. Think of the combustion engine releasing all those noxious emissions. The unbelievable benefits that it offered—faster and more convenient travel—overwhelmingly outweighed the risks that were not well understood at the time. We have been applying our best minds to create technology that has helped put men on the moon, come up with thermonuclear weapons, unravel DNA, launch satellites to beam entertainment 24/7, dive to the deepest parts of the ocean and even create a vaccine for a global pandemic. Software has been a great enabler, and while these developments also represent incredible feats of engineering, physics, biology and collaboration between disciplines, software as a tool reflects human ingenuity.

I hope that by tracing the shifts that have shaped and evolved modern software, and by searching for the key milestones of AI development in parallel, we can understand more about where we are and where we might be going. The fundamental principles behind AI are not new. Many concepts used today have been around for decades. In figure 3, I've captured a snapshot of some of the major milestones influencing technology, software and AI over time. Each of these has laid an important block as a foundation, and each block stacks positively on top of the next. There are many, many other developments that could be included, but this is a very high-level summary to show how human progress in the world of software has been rapidly increasing.

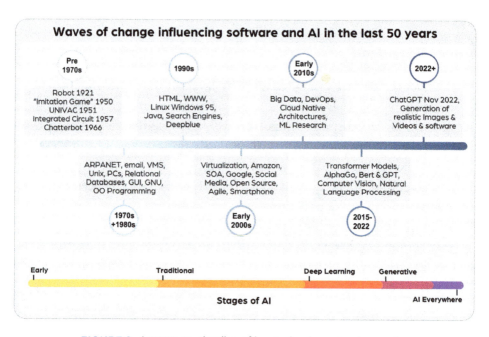

FIGURE 3. *A summary timeline of key technology developments.*

Let's take a quick tour.

1. Early AI: Pre-1970s

In 1921, Karel Čapek released a science fiction play called "Rossum's Universal Robots," which introduced the idea of artificial people. This was the first known use of the word "robot," which comes from the Czech word "robota," meaning compulsory service. In 1949, Edmund Callis wrote about a vision of the future in *Giant Brains, or Machines That Think*. He wrote, "These new machines are important. They do the work of a hundred human beings for the wages of a dozen." Small wonder that even today our media are obsessed with the theme of AI coming for our jobs.

Alan Turing's paper, "Computing Machinery and Intelligence" in 1950 sparked the first discussions on machine intelligence as a field of study. Throughout the '50s there were several developments central to the foundation of AI. Marvin Minsky created SNARC, one of the first analog implementations of a neural network. He also co-authored the book *Perceptrons: an Introduction to Computational Geometry*, where he introduced the term. Interestingly, in the book he argued about the limitations of neural networks, which turned out to be incorrect. Fortran, the programming language released in 1957, was used in scientific and engineering fields and has influenced newer languages like C and Python.

In 1958, the first integrated circuits were invented, which paved the way for modern semiconductor chips. This miniaturization of electronic components was hugely important in making it possible to create smaller devices such as personal computers, and much later, our everyday mobile devices. IBM and others were commercially successful with their mainframe technology from 1965 on, and this drove the development of several significant features, including virtual memory, multi-tasking and a modular architecture. These concepts would later be used in modern personal computer and laptop design.

2. Traditional AI: 1970s and 1980s

In 1970, ARPANET emerged as a research platform that paved the way for modern distributed networks and the internet. The first email was sent across the network using the @ symbol to separate the users name from the host address. In 1977, Digital Equipment Corporation (DEC) released VMS for their VAX minicomputers. VMS had a significant influence on modern computing by introducing principles that are still in use such as: compatibility and portability, high availability through clustering, fault tolerance and most importantly, virtual memory management which increased the amount of memory available by swapping data between a physical disk and RAM. In the '80s we witness the launch of the first relatively affordable personal computers. This creates access and awareness across all levels of society that new machines could be used to replace or augment certain types of manual work. Sounds familiar! It also marks the birth of general-purpose software applications like early spreadsheets and word processors that now have broad applicability across business and day-to-day life. Richard Stallman founded the Free Software Foundation (FSF) and the GNU Project, advocating for software that respects the user's freedom to run, study, share, and modify the code for their own purposes. This establishes an important software movement that will grow as a counterculture and offer an alternative to the larger commercial software companies at that time.

3. 1990s

Some suggest that this decade was an AI winter due to declining public interest and reduced funding. You could argue this was simply because we were too busy with other important breakthroughs. Personal computing was in high demand and it gobbled up all the attention and technology investment. The start of the '90s saw the emergence of the early commercial internet, and the first world wide web technologies: HTTP, HTML and the URL invented by Tim Berners-Lee in 1989. All of these were made available as open-source technology for anyone to use. His support for net neutrality, open access and technology development for good is a lesson we need to take forward in the future development of AI.

Linus Torvalds released the Linux kernel under the General Public License GPL. This operating system kernel was developed collaboratively by a global community and challenged proprietary operating systems and demonstrated the power of open-source development. Mosaic, the first GUI-based browser, forged the path to change the way we access, use and share information. The launch of Windows 95 was the first marketing breakthrough into popular culture and mainstream media. A global software market was born. As the internet and the web gained traction, online commerce became possible and pioneers like Amazon (1994), eBay (1995) and PayPal (1998) emerged. It was around this time the early Software as a Service (SaaS) players were founded: NetSuite and Salesforce led the way. They were successful in establishing recurring annual subscriptions using an internet browser to run the application instead of the more traditional once off license fee to install software locally on the machine.

It is also worth noting another slightly forgotten milestone in AI history. Chess was seen as a game that suited human intelligence because it required complex problem-solving, long-term strategic planning and the ability to adapt to unpredictable moves. A machine defeating a world chess champion would point to wider and future implications beyond the game. Deep Blue was a chess-playing supercomputer developed by IBM. It played the grandmaster Gary Kasparov in two sets of six games in 1996 and 97. Kasparov won the first set. Deep Blue was upgraded before the second and it defeated Kasparov 3.5-2.5. The supercomputer didn't use many aspects of modern AI, it relied on brute force computing power to work through massive combinations of different moves per second. It was still a historic moment, marking how far computers had come to that point.

4. Early 2000s

The dot.com bust between 2000 and 2002 sharpened the focus on venture capital investment in technology. Billions of dollars had been invested in early-stage companies who had no concrete business plan other than using the latest web and internet technology to create software. When the investment party came to an end, many of these start-ups failed and the resulting drop in technology spend caused huge job losses across the entire software industry. It also sharpened the minds of everyone involved in running a modern technology and software company. Survivors like Amazon, Microsoft and others would go on to significantly shape our digital lives today. Virtualization helps spark the beginning of cloud computing, probably the most transformative wave of technology in the past century. This is a hardware and software design pattern that has been used for years. It is put into use by Google, hosted on vast arrays of cheap servers, along with mapReduce and BigTable to power the scale of their new search engine. The hosting of servers at scale will eventually shift data centers from static environments to dynamic and flexible resource pools. Amazon launched EC2 (Elastic Compute Cloud) in 2006, and in 2009 Microsoft caught up with their Azure offering. Service Oriented Architecture (SOA) gains traction, with many large companies investing in more loosely-coupled software applications, with a focus on integrating the best tools together using interfaces and application programming interfaces (APIs).

No brief look at technology and AI would be complete without mentioning the iPhone. Launched in 2007, the level of engineering quality that was embodied in this miniature device set a new standard for consumer products and for software. The world moved even further into the digital spectrum. These devices will go on to have a massive influence on how we work and live, shaping how we communicate and connect to the world around us.

5. The Deep Learning Stage: 2010-2015

In this stage of AI development, we see breakthroughs in deep-learning techniques and algorithms, along with extremely large datasets and advanced computing hardware. These networks and models achieve remarkable performance across various tasks, including image recognition, speech recognition and natural language processing. Two main advances help the surge forward around this time: big data and cloud architecture.

Big data technologies allow the collection, storage and processing of very large amounts of structured and unstructured data from many different sources. A great example of a vast data source is Twitter (now X) on social media. In the early days, businesses were quick to investigate how to extract value from this platform. Brand new software called social listening applications were created to interpret when a tweet started trending in popularity. The aim of the software was to determine the sentiment being expressed and measure the impact on the company name or brand. Machine learning solutions for sentiment analysis drove an increase in investment into the space. As a result of the novelty and sheer size of the available datasets, around this time we see the role of data scientist coming to the fore, with the growing demand for data-driven insights across a range of business scenarios.

As for cloud architecture, Docker arrives in 2010 and supports the move towards microservice architecture, which features lightweight software containers. It becomes easier for software creators to continue breaking down monolithic applications into smaller independent services. In 2012, Kubernetes changes how software can be deployed. It works to orchestrate the deployment, scaling and management of these new containerized applications across clusters of machines, automating complex tasks and ensuring high availability. As a result, cloud-native architectures evolve quickly. The biggest impact of cloud computing is not just on the technology; we also see a huge change in economic and commercial models. It reshapes how businesses and consumers pay for software and how they think about and buy their computing capability. The hyperscalers emerge: Microsoft, Amazon, Oracle, Tencent, Alibaba, Google and Meta. These companies invest billions if not trillions of dollars in building data centers to cater to the global demand in computing, data processing and software as a service. In 2014, a key research paper, "Generative Adversarial Nets," proposes a new architecture to help overcome some of the challenges that machine learning models had in generating realistic text and images.

6. Generative AI: 2015-2021

In March 2016, in an event which echoes the Kasparov/Deep Blue chess showdown, DeepMind's AlphaGo wins three out of four matches in the complex game of Go against one of the highest-ranked players in the world, Lee Sodol. In 2017, a Google research team published findings on a new type of neural network architecture called a transformer model. Their legendary paper, "Attention is All You Need," demonstrates significant advancements in natural language processing, with the prospect of it having other applications in the areas of image classification, video processing and answering questions. Based on this design, OpenAI released GPT in 2018, their first language model capable of generating human-quality text. Deepmind continued to evolve their version of AlphaGo, releasing AlphaGo Zero and AlphaZero. In 2019, they published a paper describing a new algorithm they call MuZero. Based on AlphaZero, it was designed to master games without knowing their rules, and to train using self-play. In other words, it uses the experience it collects when interacting with the environment to train itself.

7. AI Everywhere: The New Era

The years 2022 and 2023 will be known as watershed years for AI. "Transformers made self-supervised learning possible, and AI jumped to warp speed," said Nvidia founder and CEO Jensen Huang in his keynote address at its Technology Conference in 2022. Although there had been various signposts along the way such as the realistic deep-fake videos popping up in social media, the human-like assistants that arrived in our homes like Alexa and Siri, it was not until the second half of 2022 and early 2023 that the world really sat up and took notice. There were a range of significant breakthroughs that made the news:

TABLE 1 – AI announcements burst on the scene

Area	Product Release, Vendor, Date and Description
Text	ChatGPT: OpenAI's revolutionary chatbot, November 2022, generates human-quality text in response to prompts and questions
	Ithaca: DeepMind's AI tool, October 2022, assists historians by identifying missing text in ancient documents using deep learning
	Bard (now called Gemini): Google response to ChatGPT, December 2022, focuses text generation on factual accuracy with search integration
	Claude 2: Anthropic's upgraded LLM, July 2023, shows improvements in code writing and support for longer responses and bigger context windows
Speech	LaMDA 3: Google, May 2022, understands and responds to natural language conversations
	Project Amber: DeepMind's technology for people with speech impairments, July 2022, translates thoughts into speech using brain-computer interfaces
Image	DALL-E 2: OpenAI's powerful image-generation model, January 2022, comes out with advanced editing features
	Midjourney: AI art platform, July 2022, allows users to create artwork by using text prompts
	Stable Diffusion: Open-source text-to-image diffusion model, July 2022, makes image generation more accessible
Video	Make-A-Video: Google's video generation model, May 2022, creates short video clips from text descriptions
	Meta's Codec Avatars for Facebook, October 2022, creates realistic avatars for video conferencing and social interactions

The new era had begun. ChatGPT became a topic of social conversation, reminding me very much of how the internet crossed over into common consciousness. Jensen Huang, in his Nvidia keynote in 2022 summarized it well, "AI is racing in every direction—new architectures, new learning strategies, larger and more robust models, new science, new applications, new industries—all at the same time." Investment into AI has exploded. It is estimated by Statista that private and corporate investment in AI has grown sixfold since 2016 and that trend will continue into the second half of the decade. This will reach and exceed a total US $120 billion investment each year.

I'm hoping by now that you are ready to ask yourself the question: "How can I take some positive steps to understand and embrace the changes that are coming?" Well, honestly, read on. This is the key to the book. I want to challenge everyone in their current role to think deeply about the topic and actively answer some of the questions posed. Take a quiet moment and write down some notes on what you think might happen based on what you now know. I like to think of myself as an optimist and I believe people are inherently good. I've also come across enough exceptions that make the rule! I must admit to being a little worried. The main source of my unease is where these investment dollars will go. Will most of it go towards removing the types of entry level jobs that would be created in emerging economies like the Philippines or in Africa? Jobs in support, administration and running routine back-office tasks. These are easy targets for AI right now. This would be a terrible shame, perhaps cutting off a vital source of income in societies that need it most. Income that would help drive powerful improvements in healthcare, children's education, equality, and more opportunities for a vast portion of the world's population. We see lots of debate about the ethics surrounding AI and I propose here that this is too general an argument, too philosophical to be meaningful. We need to start talking about how we create equality with AI and make the world a better place for every human born in the next hundred years.

What is AI? Context is King

"Hallucination is what we call it when we don't like it, creativity is what we call it when we do like it."

—MARC ANDREESSEN

The aim of this chapter is to try to explore and explain AI in plain English. It is likely you may have read about these topics elsewhere and you may remain uncertain about how the puzzle fits together. In certain sections we will go into some level of technical detail. The hope is that readers will understand and build on the concepts as we progress.

AI is the simulation of human intelligence by a machine. It is the label given to an entire field of study and technology innovation that has been active for decades. The term AI has entered popular use and covers a huge range of topics, technologies, tools and a fair bit of hype. In our definition, simulation is the key word. The software technology that AI is built on cannot really understand the world in the same way as we humans can. The software uses mathematical principles, pattern matching and statistical algorithms that have been created to perform data processing, prediction and recognition tasks. It is trained using example data, and programmed to make the best prediction of an answer to a given problem. Yes, AI is just a type of software!

The term AGI (Artificial General Intelligence) came into use in the late twentieth-century and has moved the goalposts. The definition of AGI divides opinion. We currently have no agreed set of words that defines a measurable target. I propose in simple terms that an AGI is a machine that can learn, sense and think like humans. This kind of machine is still theoretical, as the technology does not exist yet. An AGI would have to be able to sense its environment, learn without supervision, adapt this learning from a field of study and apply it to solve an unfamiliar task or problem in a completely different domain. Most experts agree that we are far from this level of machine intelligence. You could compare it to humans traveling to other planets—possible to imagine, but impossible in our lifetime. We will need several major and unforeseen breakthroughs to help us on the way to AGI—part of the solution will be to mimic how the human brain works. More on this later.

In this chapter we trace how the various solution patterns and AI technology implementations progressed from the '50s through to the present day. We look at recent new developments that have dramatically accelerated progress. The combination of cheaper and more powerful computing capabilities in the cloud along with the ability to handle vast quantities of data have really helped the forward momentum. Together, all these elements have brought AI into everyday conversation. The critical pivot point was the publication in 2017 of the now iconic Google research paper, "Attention is All You Need," on transformer models (based on an idea in a 2014 paper). The concepts and software implementation it shared with the world resulted in almost human-like performance from AI software, and propelled AI into the mainstream media. Just remember though, this is not the stuff of science fiction just yet, the new AI models are incredibly good at generating text and images, but lack any sort of AGI capability. Let's open up the box and explore the core features and functions of AI to assess its potential.

Machine Learning

Machine learning and AI are often confused as being the same thing. Machine learning is a distinct part of AI. It is the discipline of training software programs (algorithms) to read and recognize data sets, apply various input parameters and execute functions on the data. This is the process of creating what we call machine learning models. These models can predict outcomes and classify information, and they can do this without human intervention. What does one of these models look like and how are they put together? In figure 4, we have an example of the life cycle of a machine learning pipeline. It is ideal if we have a subject matter expert from the business or discipline who can guide and assist in ensuring we are solving a real world problem.

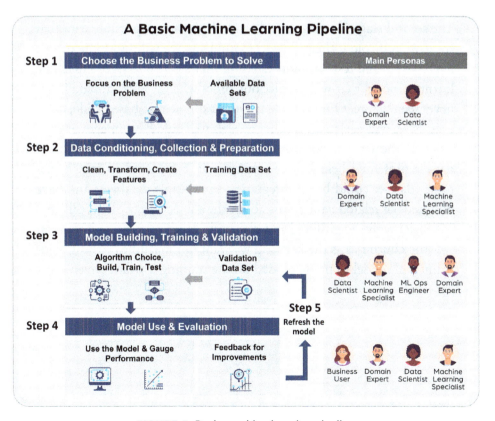

FIGURE 4. *Basic machine learning pipeline.*

Step 1. Start With a Business Problem to Solve

We will take an example from mobile telecommunications, a highly data-driven industry actively measuring all aspects of their customer relationships for many years. One important metric is "customer churn," where a customer will move to another provider at the end of their contract. In our example, we have a customer success manager who brings us a full list of his customers in a specific segment, and asks, "Can you please make a prediction on which ones are likely to churn in the coming quarter?" We have a business challenge and we will look to solve it using available data and a machine learning model.

Step 2. Data Conditioning: Collection and Preparation

The second stage is to assess, collect and prepare all possible data that we have available to help solve the problem. We will use some of this data to train and test our model. The ultimate goal is to have a machine learning model that will predict outcomes when it looks at data it has never seen before. Our example is using a simple text-based table, however, as we will see later, for other models we could have images or even video as the inputs. For our example, a summary table of customer data is presented below. More typically in a business setting, a customer dataset could be an integration of multiple databases and have hundreds of related data points about the subject. Very often, this step will also involve identifying and collecting other relevant data sources.

The churn risk is the key field we want our machine learning algorithm and model to predict based on the training it will receive.

TABLE 2 – Sample dataset for our machine learning model

Customer Age	Monthly Spend	Last Upgrade Date	Support Calls	Churn Risk Y/N
35	50	December 2022	2	N
42	60	January 2023	0	N
55	45	November 2023	0	N
21	25	June 2021	1	Y
29	35	March 2022	0	N
38	55	September 2020	5	Y
50	70	January 2020	6	Y

Note: In real scenarios, this dataset would contain hundreds of thousands of other rows of data.

Data Preparation

Raw data is rarely fully ready for a machine learning model to use. There are a number of actions that could be taken to further prepare the data. We could check for missing data, we could also convert text into numerical representations (machine learning algorithms like this notation better). We could add calculated fields to enrich the data set—this type of activity is known as "feature engineering" and benefits from having some data science skills available. An example of this in our dataset above would be to extract out a list of all the support calls for each customer from another system, then summarize the total count of calls by customer.

Separating the Data for Training and Testing

A key aspect of preparing a machine learning model is to ensure we have separate data used for training and testing. The training data will have correct answers provided alongside the model to help it learn. In our example this could be a list of historic customers who recently left the business and customers who renewed their contract so we already know the churn outcome. Our test dataset will also have correct answers, but we will hold this back until the test phase so that the model will not have seen this data before.

Step 3. Model Building, Training and Validation

In this step we assemble the software components together to form the machine learning model. Data science skills will again come to the fore. We need to choose a specific algorithm that would be suitable for predicting the customer churn risk based on the given features in our data table. In this particular example, logistic regression, decision tree or an ensemble model could be suitable. There are many options available for implementing the chosen model, the detail of which is beyond the scope of this book. (Some of the more commonly used are open-source python libraries. These are software programs written in python that can perform pre-tested pattern matching, classification and predictive functions. Some examples for anyone interested in further research would be NumPy, Pandas, Scikit-learn, TensorFlow and PyTorch.) Along with the python scripts we will include parameters and weights. These are explained a bit further in this section. The parameters and weights will typically be given default values ahead of training.

Model Training

When the software model itself is assembled and ready for training, the machine learning specialist will launch the function to read and process the training dataset. The logic in the software will execute on the training data and it will learn the patterns and relationships between the input features (age, monthly spend, last upgrade month, support calls) and the target variable (churn risk). Training time and cost can be a consideration when dealing with larger data sets. There are skills needed to examine different ways to optimize the solution design, balancing training/cost objectives with the overall accuracy of the model.

The model will learn by making its own predictions and then compare these to the actual results that were shared. It will then adjust its internal parameters and weights in a series of iterations, with the goal being to reduce the difference between the predictions and the actual outputs. There are several metrics that are used to gauge the success of the training, examples include F1 score and mean squared error. For each pass of the training, the model will calculate a loss function, which shows how well its predictions match the true outputs. The goal of training is to minimize the loss value.

Model Validation

Once we have achieved our target outcomes in training mode, we are ready to test the model. The test dataset is now played through the model to process/predict the churn risk. Data science expertise comes into play again to evaluate machine learning metrics like accuracy, precision, recall and F1 score. Understanding and interpreting these metrics requires a grasp of the meaning and implications for our specific business problem. The most important evaluation metrics are outlined in Appendix 2. Other important tasks that can be carried out here to improve the model include:

- modifying the model parameters and weights known as hyperparameter tuning (this sounds like something you might do on a spaceship, it's actually just the process of changing parameters around to try to achieve better results)

- performing further feature engineering

- considering different algorithms

Model Persistence

When we are satisfied with the performance of the model that has been assembled, we will save it so we can deploy it for use. This saving process (persistence) will create a snapshot of the model's internal state. Here are some examples to help demystify what goes on in saving a machine learning model:

- Technical parameters—weights and biases in the case of neural networks—can represent the knowledge gained during the training phase and are used to make predictions on new data.

- Sometimes the pre-processing steps that were performed as part of training will be needed in production. The details of these steps are also saved, ensuring the same preprocessing is applied to new data before making predictions.

- Any metadata is also saved. This is information that describes the type of model, the version of the algorithm and any code libraries used. This all helps in identifying and understanding the model when it is loaded up again for execution.

Step 4. Deploy and Use the Model

Deploying the model to a production environment for secure use will typically involve both the machine learning/data engineer and the DevOps team to ensure all components and parameters are configured correctly. The model can now be used to make predictions on data not seen before. In our example of customer churn, we can now take a completely new set of customers (with their age, monthly spend, customer tenure, support calls), and the model will confidently predict whether these customers are likely to churn or not.

In a real-world scenario, armed with this new information about predicted churn, a business team could design some win-back incentives for a specific set of customers, focusing on the highest spending segment. They could also choose to extend a new handset upgrade offer to a segment of younger customers and test these marketing campaigns against the churn outcomes over time.

Step 5. Refresh the Model

It is important to note that the machine learning life cycle continues even when the model is in production. It is obvious but vital to continuously measure the performance of the model and gather feedback from our business stakeholders. The performance of models can experience change over time, including the degradation of predictive capability. This is known as concept drift and can be a tricky problem to solve. One option is to completely retrain the model in batch mode with additional data, another is continual retraining with smaller datasets, providing up-to-date context to the model to allow it to keep up with shifts in the underlying data trends. Along with concept drift, business needs can also evolve, so we must be prepared to adapt and improve the model over time.

Auto Machine Learning (AutoML)

In the last couple of years, we have seen the emergence of AutoML, which is an exciting way for people to start using machine learning without having to be a data scientist. Tools such as Autogluon, DataRobot and Amazon SageMaker AutoPilot offer an automated path through the pipeline from Step 2 onwards. Not only do they abstract some of the technical details, they also have proven to be really good at choosing the right algorithms and stacking models in such a way as to outperform manual machine learning pipelines. Naturally, practitioners in machine learning will want to retain some control over these decisions. IBM Watson Studio and H20 are other examples of evolving machine learning platforms, so this entire area is already morphing into AI as a service. This abstracted level of capability and automation is what many businesses will seek as machine learning gets more widely adopted into everyday applications. Some current everyday uses of machine learning are speech to text (can be used in most smartphones to dictate a text message), voice assistants like Alexa and Siri and recommendation systems like those used in Netflix and Spotify. There are many wider examples of AI making their way into our digital world, more of which we will discuss in chapter 3.

Types of Learning

Let's move beyond the pipeline now and look at notable types of machine learning.

TABLE 3 – Types of machine learning

Type and Use	Description	Strengths	Weaknesses
Supervised Learning Predictive modeling, sentiment analysis, fraud detection	Learns patterns and relationships from curated and labeled training data	Able to make accurate predictions Can generalize well when given previously unseen data	Requires large amounts of labeled training data Can be sensitive to noise and outliers Limited application with unlabeled data
Unsupervised Learning Customer segmentation, anomaly detection	Learns patterns and relationships from unlabeled data	Is very useful when labeled data is unavailable or expensive	Evaluating performance can be challenging Prone to overfitting with complex datasets
Reinforcement Learning Decision-making tasks such as game playing Autonomous vehicle control	Learns through trial and error interactions with an environment	Capable of learning optimal actions through exploration and exploitation Optimal solution might change over time	High compute complexity and training time Requires well-defined reward signals Can lead to reward hacking where the model takes shortcuts

Type and Use	Description	Strengths	Weaknesses
Deep Learning Image classification, speech recognition, natural language processing	Uses models that aim to be like the human brain, called neural networks to process huge datasets and learn complex patterns	Can handle large-scale data Can automatically learn from raw data Excellent performance on tasks like image recognition, natural language processing and speech recognition	Requires substantial compute resources Difficult to interpret what is happening within the model compared to traditional machine learning models

Deep learning deserves special mention, as it touches on the most critical elements of AI that are relevant for this book. Deep learning is a subset of machine learning that uses neural networks to simulate aspects of how the human brain learns. Note the key words being used in this definition! The machine is trying to *simulate* aspects of how the human brain learns. A brief aside: the biological neurons in our brains can communicate with each other through electrical impulses and chemical signals. These connections form intricate circuits that facilitate sensation, movement and human cognitive functions. The brain is made up of multiple neural networks which fire in certain patterns and generate output without the brain itself really understanding what it does. It is also proposed that the human brain can reorganize its neural circuits in response to changes in sensory input and learning—this is known as neuroplasticity. The key difference between the artificial neural networks we construct for machine learning and the human brain, is that the software cannot yet recreate the magical neuroplasticity that is central to how our brain learns, retains new information and adapts our conscious behavior. It is inevitable that we will eventually see AGI in a machine. Technologists will figure out solutions to the challenge of simulating the neuroplasticity of the brain. More on this later.

The Path to Generative AI

Steve Jobs once said, "You can't connect the dots looking forward; you can only connect them looking backwards." It is possible for us to join some dots and look at the trajectory of the critical capabilities that enabled our current phase of machine learning in AI.

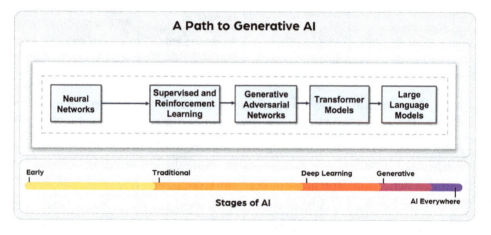

FIGURE 5. *A path to generative AI.*

I propose that the following developments define the key steps along the path to where we are today. They contribute strongly to the generative models that have taken the world by storm and led us into this new era of AI.

1. Neural networks (1957)

2. Supervised and reinforcement learning (1980s)

3. Generative adversarial networks (2014)

4. Transformer models (2017)

5. Large Language models (2018)

You may wish to skip over some of the detail, the section is intended to help de-mystify what is going on under the hood.

1. Neural Networks

Neural networks are types of deep machine learning models that take in data, receive training and predict outcomes. They are quite different to some of the other machine learning models in how they achieve this process. The purpose of this book is not to be a definitive technical reference, so I will use a very simple example to illustrate this type of solution for anyone who is not a data scientist! The simplest form of neural network is shown in figure 6.

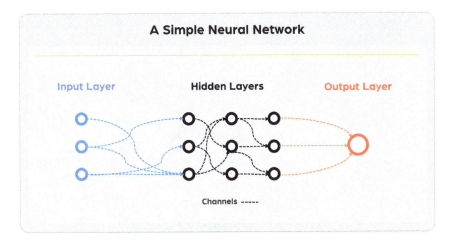

FIGURE 6. *A simple neural network.*

Neural networks are:

a) set up in computer code as layers of interconnected artificial neurons (called "perceptrons" to distinguish them from the biological neurons we have in our brain. Each perceptron can learn from training data. This is achieved by adjusting the weights and biases of the perceptrons, a concept explained a little later)

b) arranged in layers—an input layer, usually many hidden layers, and an output layer

c) connected by channels, connections between the nodes that have to be deliberately created

Remember these are constructs modeled in software code and use mathematical equations and functions. They are not little brain cells sitting in a glass jar in a lab! What is the heart of this network? The neuron, or (more precisely) the perceptron.

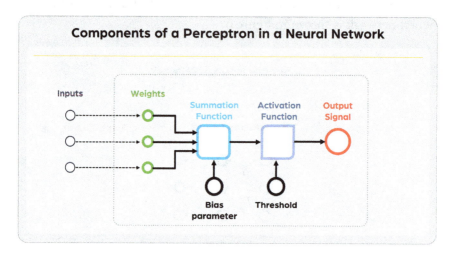

FIGURE 7. *Components of a perceptron.*

Components of a Perceptron

Inputs—A perceptron is programmed to take in a set of values called inputs. These inputs can be anything from pixels in an image to words in a message to numeric values of a credit card transaction.

Weights—Each input is given a weight, which is a number that represents the importance of that particular input.

Summation Function—This function takes the weighted sum of its inputs and adds a bias. The bias parameter is a constant value that is added to the weighted sum.

Activation function—The activation function is logic that runs using the results from the summation function (weighted sum of the inputs and bias). This function determines the output. Depending on the type of function, the output can be 1 or 0, a value between 1 and 0 or a value between -1 and 1.

The capabilities of the neural network provide a powerful framework for learning from data, for modeling complex relationships in the data and making intelligent decisions about how to process the data. They have been foundational in the development of AI and underpin many of the successful applications we see in use today.

2. Supervised and Reinforcement Learning

Both have been key drivers in how modern machine learning models have evolved. Supervised learning provides the initial capacity to map and mimic patterns in data, while reinforcement learning helps shape and refine the outputs to appear more realistic. In supervised learning, the algorithm receives labeled data that contains both the inputs (features) and the correct outputs (labels). We train the model to learn the mappings between the inputs and outputs so that it can accurately predict the output for data that it has not seen before.

Reinforcement learning trains the software using rewards for positive actions and penalties for negative actions. The objective is to maximize the rewards over time by learning which actions in given situations lead to the best outcomes. These learning techniques have been deployed in the game-playing agents like AlphaGo that helped achieve their high profile breakthroughs. There are other interesting techniques used in reinforcement learning in particular:

Real-World Interaction

Agents can interact with the real world through sensors receiving real-time feedback. This allows them to learn directly from their environment, like a robot navigating physical space or a drone learning to fly.

Simulation Environments

This is where the agents learn in a simulated environment, created for various scenarios. A good example is controlling a car in a virtual driving simulator.

Offline Learning

Models can learn from pre-recorded data known as offline learning. This data can come from various sources, such as historical logs of user interactions or sensor data collected from real-world systems.

Multi-Agent Reinforcement Learning

This approach involves training multiple agents to interact and sometimes cooperate or compete. This can be relevant for tasks like collaborative robots or training AI opponents for games. Reinforcement learning from human feedback (RLHF) is the technique that uses human intervention in the process of learning. The human feedback helps refine the outputs to better align with human expectations and preferences, improving aspects like:

- creativity and coherence—the model can learn to generate engaging and interesting content

- context and relevance—the model can better understand and respond to specific prompts and contexts

- social awareness—the model can adjust its tone and style based on the situation and intended audience

RLHF is often used in scenarios where it is harder to clearly define the outcome. An example is where scientists can provide feedback on simulated drug molecules, confirming their properties and potential effectiveness. Another example is in AI models that perform image and video processing like color correction or noise reduction. Humans can provide feedback on the edited content, indicating whether it improves the overall quality and realism.

3. Generative Adversarial Networks (GANs)

GANs are another important piece in our puzzle that has enabled the latest surge in generating realistic content, video and images. Ian Goodfellow and others proposed this first in a research paper in 2014. In the paper, they proposed an architecture featuring two deep neural networks, the generator network and the discriminator network. It was explicitly designed to overcome previous issues that were encountered in trying to use these models to generate high quality outputs like text, images and video. The architecture worked by passing random noise through a multilayer perceptron (the generator) and the discriminative model, also a multilayer perceptron.

The networks were trained to play a game against each other (hence the name adversarial) where the generator creates new data, and the discriminator (or critic) makes predictions on whether the output is real or has been generated. During the training process, the generator is working repeatedly to trick the critic, while the critic is designed using algorithms and training to predict when it is being fooled. Goodfellow and his team built a successful model that achieved very promising outputs with way less computing power. The other benefits of these GANs:

- After the initial input, a GAN can continue to train itself by producing more training data.

- The network can produce data output very efficiently and can replace hours of manual human work.

- It works to improve the quality of output data through comparison and making corrections.

GANs are now being used to generate realistic creative content, particularly in areas like image and video generation and text to image translation.

4. Transformer Models

With the paper "Attention is All You Need," published in 2017, the transformer model architecture was made available. Figure 8 shows a simplified diagram of a transformer model.

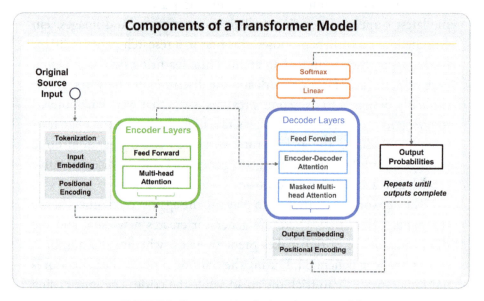

FIGURE 8. *Components of a transformer model*

Highlighted in the green and blue boxes are the feed forward neural networks. These are the same type of trained neural networks we discussed earlier. We can see that the transformer model architecture has added some further complexity:

- Encoders: The encoder processes the entire input sequence, capturing the position of the words and the relationships between words. This encoded information is then passed to the decoder, which will try to generate an output sequence one token at a time.

- Attention Mechanisms: The multi-head, self-attention mechanism weighs the importance of each input segment relative to the others. The best analogy to think of here is a bunch of detectives considering a case where each detective represents an "attention head" and works to solve a specific clue. The multi-head aspect is all the detectives collaborating in a coordinated way to help solve the overall puzzle.

- Decoders: It receives intelligent inputs from the encoder, such as the position of the words in the sequence. This gives the decoder context and helps it predict better outputs. The masked, multi-head attention design does not allow the model to get ahead of itself. It focuses on predicting just the next token or piece of output. This makes sure our detectives can't just wildly guess the outcome of the case without having all the clues examined.

Large Language Models (LLMs)

Large language models are large-scale, pre-trained, statistical language models based on neural networks. The architecture of an LLM can vary. The most popular and powerful ones we know of today such as GPT (OpenAI), LLaMA (Meta) and PaLM (Google) all use some form of the transformer model that we just explored. One way to understand what is going on inside an LLM is to ask it a question and ask it to explain how it produced the answer! I used the following example prompt in ChatGPT 3.5.

"I will provide you with a question. Can you (a) provide an answer, then (b) outline in understandable terms how you address answering the question, referring to the main aspects of your architecture and implementation and give specific examples of the question and how you build the answer? Here is the question [I would like to know the best time to visit Japan].

Here is ChatGPT's response:

Certainly! Let's proceed with the provided question:

Question:
"I would like to know the best time to visit Japan."

a) Answer: "The best time to visit Japan depends on your preferences. If you enjoy cherry blossoms, spring (March to May) is ideal. For pleasant weather, consider autumn (September to November). Keep in mind that summer can be hot and humid, while winter offers a different charm with festivals and snow. What type of experience are you looking for?

b) Explanation: Understanding the question: The user is seeking information about the best time to visit Japan.

- Tokenization—tokenization breaks down the input into smaller units, like words.

- For example, tokens: ["I", "would," "like," "to," "know," "the," "best," "time," "to," "visit," "Japan,"]

- Context awareness—considering the context window, I look at the recent conversation history to understand the user's query better.

  - Transformer model magic—The transformer model has learned from extensive text data during training, making it proficient in understanding language and context.

  - Attention mechanism—The attention mechanism lets the model focus on important words. For instance, it pays attention to "best time" and "visit Japan" when forming a response.

  - Memory of patterns—The model has learned patterns, such as associating "best time" with factors like weather, events or seasons in the context of travel.

  - Generating a response—Considering the context and patterns, the model generates a response that aims to provide helpful information about the best time to visit Japan.

- Natural language generation—The response is crafted in a way that sounds natural and coherent, aligning with how humans would communicate.

In this example, the response is tailored to the user's question, considering various factors like seasons and user preferences. The model's ability to understand context, use self-attention and generate human-like responses contributes to its effectiveness in addressing diverse queries."

If we show this in a diagram, we can see (in a very simplified way) how the LLM architecture approaches the problem and breaks down the input text into tokens. It then moves on to assembling a prediction of a trained, realistic, human-like response *one word at a time*, but all the while including the context of the words contained in the overall request.

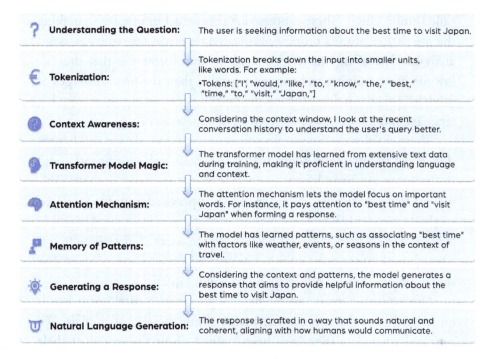

FIGURE 9. *How an LLM addresses a prompt.*

If I make a controversial statement to oversimplify the architecture such as "LLMs are just a multi-threaded recursive prediction function," there is some truth to this. It is correct to say they are multi-threaded, as the transformer architecture has multiple "threads" or attention heads. Each head focuses on different parts of the input sequence, much like having multiple perspectives analyzing the text simultaneously. The LLM does operate somewhat recursively, processing text sequentially with the output from one step becoming the input for the next step. This means the model's prediction at each point is influenced by what it has learned from the previous parts of the text. The core task of LLM when answering a text based question is to predict the next most likely word or token given an input sequence.

This is a large oversimplification though! LLMs are not just about prediction. They are also trained in tasks like summarization, translation and question answering. This means that the model has developed complex representations of language beyond just prediction. In their execution, LLMs convert words into dense numerical representations called embeddings. These capture rich contextual information, making the prediction process more sophisticated than just raw word-by-word analysis. One of the main advantages of transformers is that they allow for more training to happen in parallel than the previous types of models. This has helped reduce the cost of pre-training these very big language models on massive amounts of source text data.

There are also the fine-tuning aspects where foundation models are then given training with additional data to help with specific tasks, and this training results in higher performance in a specialist domain. This will be achieved using a combination of supervised and unsupervised methods, e.g. RLHF and instruction prompt tuning. A good example is MedPaLM2. It scored 86.5 percent on the MedQA dataset which is a benchmark of six open question answering datasets spanning professional medical exams, research and consumer queries.

Due to commercial and intellectual property restrictions, it is still quite hard to make specific statements about the size of models. We can't tell what data they have been trained on or the extent of their training to draw any comparisons between models. The capability of the model is usually depicted in terms of parameters and not in the size of the training text, even though they are indirectly related. For example, a version of GPT3 is estimated to have 175 billion parameters. The common parameters in LLMs include weights in neural networks, biases, and hyperparameters that control the learning.

TABLE 4 – Popular machine learning model sizes compared

Family	Model	Parameters	Trained Tokens
GPT	GPT3	175 billion	300 billion
	GPT4	1.76 trillion	13 trillion
LlaMA	LLaMA2	70 billion	2 trillion
PaLM	PaLM2	340 billion	3.6 trillion
Google	Gemini	3.25 billion	*Not available*

Can we compare the human brain to the more powerful LLMs that are being announced lately? The brain is estimated to have over 85 billion neurons and 100 trillion connections between them. These neurons perform different functions based on the part of the brain they are in. If we further consider the organic and dynamic nature of the brain and the rich sensory domain that it can manage, even the most powerful LLMs at this stage of AI development are not coming close to this level of complexity. Unfortunately, there are no standard formulas available to calculate the number of neurons in our machine learning models. The specific architecture and design choices of each LLM will significantly influence the number of neurons used.

If we cannot compare apples to apples, is there any way of comparing a large language model to a human? One interesting perspective can be gained from Marion Blank's research into learning at the preschool age. She examined how young children develop language and thinking skills and identified four levels of abstraction. Over the years this has been adapted and extended and can now be expressed in six levels:

1. Pre-language: This level involves the pre-verbal stage where children understand basic concepts and gestures but have not yet developed verbal language skills.

2. Emergent language: At this level, children begin to use single words or short phrases to express basic needs and ideas.

3. Concrete language: Children at this level can comprehend and produce simple sentences, focusing on concrete objects and actions.

4. Abstract language: This level involves the ability to understand and use language to describe abstract concepts, make predictions and discuss hypothetical situations.

5. Metalinguistic language: Children at this level can think and talk about language itself, including grammar rules, word meanings and language structure.

6. Pragmatic language: The highest level involves the ability to use language effectively in social contexts, including understanding and following behavioral cues, taking turns in conversations and using language to influence and achieve goals through communication.

At the time of writing, a child aged six would outperform the most powerful LLMs. Some key differences are that children develop an understanding through physical interaction with the world and complex social cues. They will process massive amounts of sensory input including sight, smell, sound and touch along with sense of space, and combine these experiences with language to form memories and reasoning capabilities. Without the sensory input, an LLM completely lacks this embodied experience, which limits their understanding of the nuances of the rich universe we live in. A child will learn language purposefully to communicate and connect with other humans and the world around them. LLMs process language for patterns and generate output in response to a question. It has no inherent drive for social connection. As children develop through their lives, they understand that others have different thoughts and perspectives. LLMs occasionally mimic this, but as of now they concretely do not possess any theory of mind. I asked the leading LLMs to rank themselves on the scale above and they answered as follows:

ChatGPT - Level 4

"While I excel in abstract language comprehension and production, my capabilities are limited to processing and generating text based on the input provided, without true understanding or awareness like a human being."

Gemini - Level 4

"I'd place myself primarily at the abstract language level, with strong capabilities in pragmatic language and a growing presence in metalinguistic language."

Mistral (a model developed in France)

"As a highly advanced, AI language model, I would rank myself at the highest level of pragmatic language. I am capable of understanding and using language effectively in various social contexts, following social cues, taking turns in conversations and utilizing language to achieve specific communicative goals. Additionally, I possess strong metalinguistic capabilities, enabling me to think and talk about language itself, including grammar rules, word meanings and language structure. I am also proficient in handling abstract language, allowing me to understand and discuss complex concepts, make predictions and engage in hypothetical situations." You have to love the European sense of humility in Mistral.

3

The Impact on Software

> *"AI is not just about machines. It's about intelligence, and intelligence is very multifaceted. It's about perception, reasoning, learning, and cognitive skills."*
>
> **—YANN LECUN**

AI is already having a profound effect on every aspect of software design and behavior. Marc Andresson said in 2011 that "software will eat the world." What he meant was that large parts of the economy would be driven by the latest software platforms and applications, and he was largely correct. We have seen an explosion in software of every type, how it has enabled new marketplaces, how it has transformed the world of healthcare, transportation, retail, manufacturing, communications and business management.

Let's begin our exploration of the impact of AI on modern enterprise business software across three broad groups.

These groups are:

1. SaaS Natives

2. SaaS Followers

3. Not SaaS—Legacy On Premises

SaaS Natives

The key characteristics of software that fall into this category would be:

- created using a cloud-native architecture for scaling and security

- microservices and API-based

- product features released often (daily or weekly)

- automated testing built into the delivery cycle

- depth of used feature set is low to medium

- complexity of UI low, inline guided training

- use cases are bound to low complexity for usability

- multi-tenant and can serve many users simultaneously

- designed to be delivered and consumed as an online service

Good examples in this segment would be Monday.com, Zoom, Hubspot, Netflix, Slack and Salesforce.

Impact of AI

It may be obvious, but this will be the segment where AI capabilities will be adopted first. Many of these platforms already have basic forms of machine learning in their architecture. This makes it straightforward to plan and implement the plugging in of APIs to layer in AI support for business scenarios. For some companies in this segment, it will offer a chance to pivot their offering. There is a heck of a lot of early-stage SaaS businesses out there (launched roughly between 2019 and 2024) whose core offering is a set of features related to business process automation. These will be under most threat and I predict that we will see a very strong herd mentality develop, with moves to pivot being taken by many of these companies in the same way that Intercom has. This will also be driven by investors such as private equity, with any business going for Series B, C and other funding rounds. There will be a fundamental need for AI to be part of the longer-term story.

I would rate this segment as AI-ready but advise decision makers not to delay in assessing the strategic impact. They should begin now to fold in AI skill sets into their teams to infuse the thinking into the entire software creation process, and review all existing use cases with a critical eye. The ideal customer profile (ICP) and the product market fit that the business is based on will need to be reassessed, tweaked and proven again with the possible new AI capabilities. Enabling an AI feedback loop or "data flywheel" is readily possible in this segment. This is the concept of considering all aspects of user engagement and behavior, then feeding this through the AI model performance. The goal is to enhance the model or models and by extension the business value being offered by the application or platform. The proposed benefits cause even more user engagement and an increase in available data. This cycle goes in a virtuous circle. More users and customers, better models, more revenue.

SaaS Followers

Our second segment contains the following characteristics:

- born in a traditional on-premise architecture like MVC, NTier or SOA

- re-engineered into cloud, microservice and API design, or on a migration path towards a fully cloud-native architecture

- hosted in the cloud, will use some cloud application services

- product feature release cadence constrained due to monolithic code bases

- depth of used feature set high

- complexity of UI medium to high

- may still bear some characteristics of their on-premise origins which may limit flexibility/adaptability

I would propose the following as good examples here: Microsoft Office, Adobe, most HCM and ERP suites like UKG, Workday, Oracle, SAP and Ceridian.

Impact of AI

I would rate this segment as partially AI-ready, but with significant work to do. I would recommend that decision-makers in this segment consider one of the engagement channels such as customer support, and adopt AI there first by buying a tool that already has the capability.

Decision-makers in this segment should be ruthless in assessing features that are not going to be a core part of the application or platform in three years' time and strongly consider dropping the bottom 20 percent of the least-used features. They should use AI to identify unused areas of the monolithic codebase and use this time as a call to arms to invest more in data management and data modeling skills. Because many software teams have been obsessed with their application code for far too long, they should consider identifying a part of the application that is already on the roadmap for refactoring, and instead of repeatedly putting this off, take a small new team and take an AI-first approach. Run a series of spikes or short sprints to see how fast they can progress with AI tools and models.

Software architects and product managers need to start looking out three years from now and make investment decisions based on where demand is going to be, just as much as where the demand is or has been in the recent past. Customers will eventually want to see AI deeply embedded in the business process, so it's wise to ask them where they see the value. Hiring the right AI skill sets (knowledge of data science and machine learning) into all teams to infuse AI thinking across the software creation process will be fundamental.

3. Not SaaS—Legacy on Premises

Our third segment is the set of applications and platforms that are installed and managed on internal infrastructure. These systems offer a high degree of control and security, but they will lack the flexibility and innovation potential of the other two segments. Their characteristics include:

- born in a legacy architecture (older languages or operating systems)

- investment to re-engineer does not make business sense at this point

- can be hosted with IaaS

- product feature release cadence constrained/sometimes even not possible

- depth of used feature set low

- complexity of UI very high (requires local install)

- low automated testing

Examples here would be older ERP systems like custom-built workflow or operational systems.

Impact of AI

I would rate this segment as under significant threat from AI. I would recommend any decision-makers in this segment to figure out if there is any viable retention strategy at all. If it is impossible to replace the system in the next one to three years, they should explore if a new UI, user experience or workflow layer could be deployed on top of the legacy codebase that will be able to offer a stronger, more flexible user experience.

There will be an opportunity to procure AI-enabled applications to support non-core channels such as customer support and adopt AI there first. I understand that some major players in this segment will choose to sweat applications or platforms embedded in specialist customer bases that could be sticky, but rest assured the shift in functional demands from customers will become pressing. They will be buying into future AI-enabled ecosystems, which means that churn will be a major threat in this segment.

Impact on Software—Order of Effects

Inspired by an article on chiefmartec.com and borrowing from chemistry (where they measure order of effects in chemical reactions), the concept of zero, first and second order impacts has been widely adopted across biology, physics, engineering and business. It's an analogy we can use to examine the impact of AI on software.

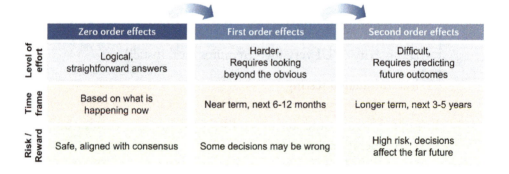

FIGURE 10. *AI impact, order of effects on software.*

Zero Order Effects—Happening Right Now

The zero-day effects are surfacing quickly. As I write this, important announcements from brand new startups to the major players are happening daily in the field of generative AI. The ability of these networks and models to generate text and images from a chat-based prompt for free has caused a lot of excitement and fear. It is the sheer quality and speed at which these outputs are generated that has made people sit up and take notice. The immediate impacts of the direct use of these tools on the world of software will follow the principles of evolution: adapt or be left behind.

I foresee that many people in the software profession will sit on the sidelines for now. There is so much happening on a weekly basis that it is difficult to choose a preferred tool, path, vendor or architecture to incorporate into the business or the software application/platform that they work on. Keeping up-to-date with announcements will mean that senior product managers, software architects and decision-makers will have to invest considerable time in research and reading at the cost of efficiency in ongoing business-as-usual activities. On the flip side, businesses that are ready and willing to invest time and effort into bringing AI into their tactical planning and execution will naturally adapt faster. I watched with interest how Irish company Intercom reacted to ChatGPT's initial launch.

FIGURE 11. *Intercom reacting to the launch of ChatGPT.*

From this initial tweet in 2022 (fig. 12), Intercom released its first AI-powered chatbot in March 2023.

FIGURE 12. *Six months on, Intercom has innovated quickly.*

Intercom then rapidly pivoted into the "only AI-powered customer service platform you need." This highlights that rapid AI innovation will occur particularly in younger SaaS companies and startups. For them, moving fast is a source of competitive advantage and viewed also as a matter of survival. There are hugely compelling reasons to embrace AI and find ways to outperform larger companies that will be slower to adapt. In 2024, Intercom announced a €100m investment into their own AI model for customer support called Fin X. They are clearly all in on this wave, with their founders professing very publicly that in order to win with AI there is no room for comfort, complacency or mediocrity.

Above the Line Versus Below the Line

AI and machine learning as a technology is already prevalent in certain industries and is being applied both above the line (interacting with human users) and below the line (embedded unseen in the application). In figure 13 we suggest some use cases and where they align.

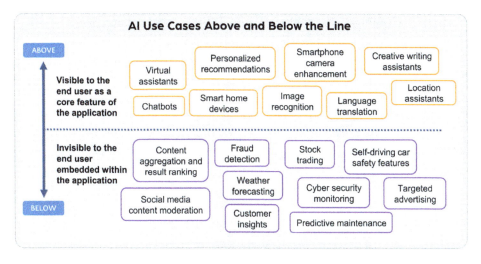

FIGURE 13. *AI use cases above and below the line.*

It helps if we take some example software brands that appear above the line (where AI is visible to the user):

- Google Maps, 2005. Uses the python-based tool called TensorFlow for traffic prediction. Real-time traffic updates and optimal route suggestions are based on historical and current data.

- Netflix, 2006. Uses Apache Spark ML for content recommendation. This improved the user experience by providing personalized movie and TV show recommendations based on the subscribers' viewing history and preferences.

- Spotify, 2008. Leverages Scikit-learn for music recommendation. Besides the breakthrough streaming of music, it also offered personalized playlists and music recommendations based on listening history and preferences.

- Grammarly, 2009, deploys custom ML models for writing assistance. This tool enhances the user's grammar and makes suggestions to improve their writing style.

- Duolingo, 2011, uses custom ML Models for language processing and the learning journey. The end user receives adapted exercises and feedback as they progress through their personal learning path.

- Apple, 2014. Machine learning models are used for activity tracking. The model can detect and track when the wearer of the Apple Watch engages in physical activities like walking, running and cycling.

And below the line (AI is invisible to the user):

- C3.ai 2009. C3 AI suite powers predictive maintenance. It reduces downtime and maintenance costs by predicting equipment failures and scheduling proactive maintenance.

- SmartNews, 2012. Uses adaptive machine learning for news aggregation.

- The subscriber receives only the top-rated news recommendations from across an enormous array of news sources based on their stated interests and preferences.

- Qualtrics (Clarabridge), 2017. Uses machine learning and NLP for customer experience management. The application ingests and provides insights and recommended actions on events such as call center conversations, chat logs, survey responses, social media posts and product reviews.

- Tesla, 2015. Leverages custom AI and machine learning algorithms to power their autonomous driving capability. They promise advanced driver assistance systems and self-driving technology, but this has been error prone and has failed to live up to early hype.

Near-Term Effects

The first order effects during 2024 and 2025 will be a combination of including commodity AI features into all aspects of the software stack, along with generative AI being used more and more in the creation and management of the software. This will be mostly achieved by exposing machine learning capabilities and features through APIs. Here is a simplified view of how machine learning models will be integrated into the software architecture using APIs.

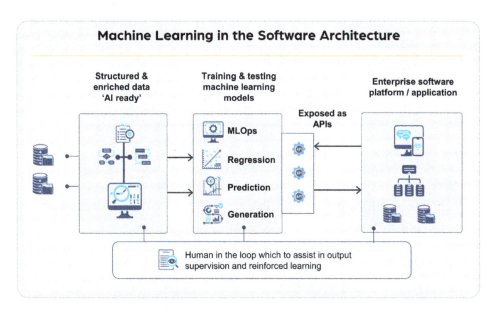

FIGURE 14. *Machine learning consumed as a service.*

Right now, much of the software that is in use in the world has been designed by two sets of qualified experts working together, one in the technical domain and the other in business. These two groups work together to interpret real-world problems and create solutions using a myriad of combinations of design patterns and technology components. The emergence of low code and no code platforms has changed the approach, reducing the amount of technical expertise required and the amount of software code that is written to solve a problem.

TABLE 5 – Comparison of Low code and No Code software platforms

Feature	Low Code	No Code
Target user	Developers, those with some technical knowledge	Business users, nontechnical individuals
Coding needed	Minimal coding for complex customizations	No coding required
Customization	High degree of customization	Limited to what the platform offers
Speed of development	Faster than traditional coding	Fastest option
Use cases	Complex applications, integrations	Simpler applications, process automation

Table 5 explores some of the key features of these platforms, and they claim they can reduce the barrier to entry so domain specialists can create their own software solutions. In practice they have achieved a decent penetration in certain use cases and industries. Somewhat surprisingly, these platforms have not massively replaced existing software tools; rather, they are catering to the more flexible needs of users in personal productivity scenarios. In this phase, it is highly likely that AI-generated code will be limited to the lower end of complexity.

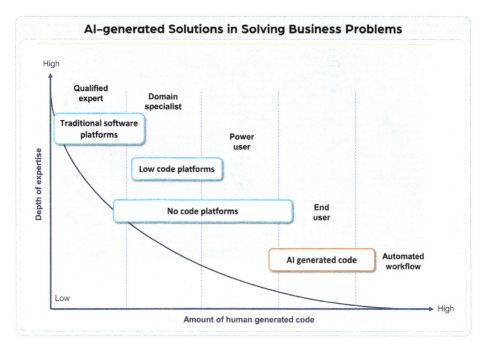

FIGURE 15. *Types of software platforms.*

On March 12 2024, Cognition AI announced Devin, the world's first AI software engineer.

Cognition ✓
@cognition_labs

Today we're excited to introduce **Devin, the first AI software engineer.**

Devin is the new state-of-the-art on the SWE-Bench coding benchmark, has successfully passed practical engineering interviews from leading AI companies, and has even completed real jobs on Upwork.

Devin is an autonomous agent that solves engineering tasks through the use of its own shell, code editor, and web browser.

When evaluated on the **SWE-Bench** benchmark, which asks an AI to resolve GitHub issues found in real-world open-source projects, Devin correctly resolves 13.86% of the issues unassisted, far exceeding the previous state-of-the-art model performance of 1.96% unassisted and 4.80% assisted.

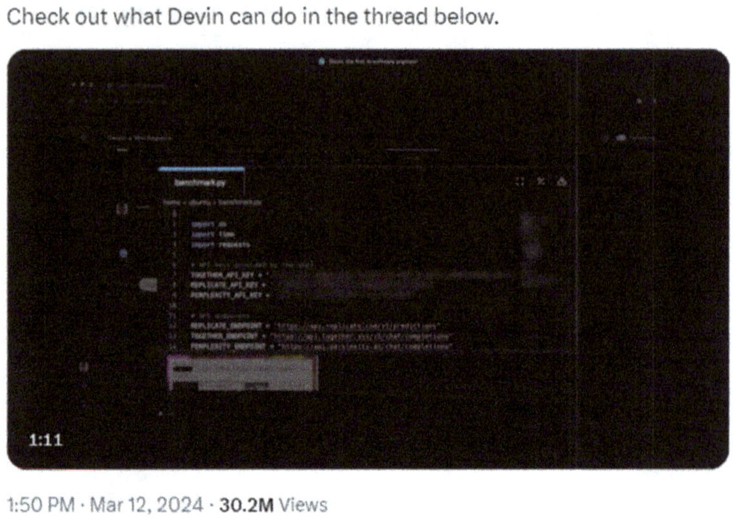

Check out what Devin can do in the thread below.

1:50 PM · Mar 12, 2024 · **30.2M** Views

FIGURE 16. *Cognition announcing their AI software engineer, Devin.*

Cognition said Devin was created so that "engineers can now focus on more complex and innovative problems while Devin AI efficiently takes care of more routine coding tasks." This tool is quite new and far from complete. Cognition claims to have achieved a large increase in accuracy in the number of defects fixed in a widely recognized benchmark test. Apparently, Devin resolves 13 percent of the issues, and by comparison GPT4 was able to resolve just 2 percent of the issues. The software engineering community has been quick to find flaws and holes in the claims made by Cognition for Devin. The ability to debug simple errors seems to be its main strength, which leaves it very far away from being an autonomous engineer. It is safe to say that right now Devin is simply an early version of a decent programming assistant.

Enter AI. Now the game is changing. We can chat conversationally with a machine. Instructions or questions can be given in plain English, we don't need to worry about structured software commands or how precise the question is. A software developer can use all the power of generative AI to create software in a less structured way of working, with fewer constraints.

Creation of a New Category

We can also see a new category emerging, AI-first software. The characteristics of this segment will build on the SaaS-native attributes, but with AI capabilities at their core from the very beginning. We will see:

- machine learning models consumed at all levels of the stack through APIs

- specialist models trained on custom domain datasets offering strong value in tightly-defined use cases

- data streaming/processing being considered for AI use cases

- workflow, user interfaces and GUIs will be enabled with intelligent user feedback features driven from learning models

- multi-channel and multi-modal user experiences can be supported by AI as a service, not all models will have to be built in house

Not all of the software will be based on AI or have machine learning components, but those that are will be planned and seamlessly integrated into the architecture in ways that will force change in how software is designed. Early examples are OpenAI, Jasper, Perplexity, DeepL, Runway and Casca.

Here are some predicted effects we will see over the 2024 and 2025 time horizon.

TABLE 6 – Impacts on software in the near term horizon

Area	Impact
Engagement channels and UI	Virtual assistants, natural language and conversational UIs will be integrated back into any readily applicable datasets. This should enable the chatbot/UI to be ready and prepared to answer unforeseen contextual questions with accurate information and strong responses. New users will continue to be offered personalization, at the cost of giving up their data. Classic web search will continue to be disrupted but will remain relevant as a statement of record helping to validate against LLM hallucinations.
Application, business logic and workflow	Opportunity for applications and platforms to feed all available usage pattern data, error/failure logs, workflow performance into models that will reflect real-time performance feedback. This will be used as a CoPilot capability for all sorts of routine scenarios. Applications like Outlook, LinkedIn, Facebook and TikTok that can gain wider access to other application graphs will become much more proactive and meaningful. These applications will be able to accept a prompt and the conversational layer will respond with recommended actions which can be accepted and executed in-line.
Service and orchestration layer	Obvious to state perhaps, but AI models will be exposed and consumed as APIs like a commodity as part of the infrastructure. Finance operations will be interested in tracking usage and real return on investment however, some of these off-the-shelf models will not be cheap to use or train with internal data. Tools to track and safely remove unused elements of a code base in applications or platforms will become much more powerful. This will solve a major headache of technology sprawl, leading to leaner delivery models for cloud-native software owners.
Data processing and storage	Existing data sources, both structured and unstructured, will be shared with AI models specializing in assessment and pre-processing. These models will accept a use case as a target goal, and then recommend how to enhance the datasets and suggest ways to get more value from the data. This enrichment cycle will increase demand for both data and model marketplaces. The new capabilities will stretch data and privacy laws very quickly, which will have to play catch up in the same way as GDPR did with big data.

Area	Impact
Infrastructure	Infrastructure as code will see new tools emerge that are informed and managed by AI "control tower" type applications. Control towers will receive data from every layer of the software stack, and we can predict they will quickly become capable of intervening before bottlenecks and major outages happen in the architecture.

Data Privacy and Security Impacts

Along with the characteristics of the software, there will be a major impact on the trust and privacy concerns of customers and end users. Before GDPR, companies played fast and loose with personal data. It was only when the legislative frameworks came into force that businesses took data security and privacy seriously. The subsequent levying of serious fines by the regulators created a financial business case to invest in controls, tools and measures to protect data. End users and consumers are also much more informed nowadays and are empowered to be more discerning about what data they are prepared to share. Yes, they want software to be quicker, better and more personalized for them, but they also want it to be completely safe. Providers that do not value data privacy, trust and integrity will be boycotted or avoided. Some of the key challenges for those involved in designing security into their platforms will be:

- Support for the right to be forgotten within trained machine learning models will require trust.

- Using customer data to fine tune models will need deep technical explanation and assurances.

- Being able to explain to end users how their data is being used and why will become seriously important.

- Adhering to new regulatory frameworks like Dora may impact the ability to go to market with advanced or cutting-edge models.

Many of the data privacy challenges up to now have been when personal identifiable data was breached by accident, or by humans not following the correct process. There will have to be specific rules and tools created to monitor AI models and networks to ensure no data leakage or misuse occurs. I can see a new feature set being built for data privacy which will validate a model design and reflect if it is consistent with the specific permissions that exist or what fair business use would permit.

Longer-Term Effects

The longer-term second order effects will be felt in two or three annual budget cycles, when businesses make the decision to decisively fund the acquisition of AI tools or develop the capabilities in house. Many companies will do both. We can easily see end users subscribing to their own specific AI tools in the same way as the BYOD (bring your own device) phase of Office IT happened when smartphones and iPads/tablets became hugely popular after 2010. It is going to quickly become very hard to differentiate software offerings due to basic AI feature proliferation. The major software vendors like Microsoft, Amazon, IBM and others will be able to heavily invest at scale, going all in on data, compute power, training and leveraging the power of their user graphs to offer deep personalization. We are already seeing this in the tie up between Microsoft and OpenAI. It will be a natural progression to see CoPilot sit alongside every Microsoft 365 user nudging, guiding and helping with everyday productivity challenges. The depth of data that will be available to assist these AI tools in personalizing the experience is already huge. CoPilot will be able to observe all your behavior on SharePoint, Outlook, Word, Excel and PowerPoint, going back possibly years and offering you unbelievable insights about how you work and how you can be more effective and efficient. If this can be done safely and securely, then most people will embrace it automatically.

A second order effect that I propose here in the usage of software will be where the application itself will have intelligence built in to adapt and tailor workflows to the needs of a specific user. The application will be learning constantly from user behavior, monitoring the quality of outcomes, tracking failure rates and nudging the user along the correct path. It should even be able to intervene in a workflow to avoid a major failure like a data breach. Applications and platforms will ultimately provide insight on when best to deploy new features or remove features depending on the user's skill and needs.

For those who buy a lot of their software for their businesses, the power of choice will almost be a burden. How will they benchmark or assess one expert model from another? How will they substantiate a vendor's claims that they can instantly integrate AI into existing products and workflows? Procuring software with AI capabilities will mean that software architects will have to be given a seat at the decision table of the buying team. Assessing the market for a new HCM or CRM suite, finance or ERP platform will become a more significant business choice than ever. Choosing a vendor will be choosing an ecosystem not just for support and application integration, but for their AI capabilities now, future AI roadmap and associated data privacy and security pledges. For those who build software, committing to open-source or closed-source models will be a tough choice. What models to choose and how to source and hire staff with the right AI skills will become strategic objectives in 2025 and 2026.

Let's drop into a case study to tease out an example of how AI will impact decision-making around the classic "buy versus build" decisions that many businesses will face in this new era.

CASE STUDY – AI for Customer Management

Scenario

A large enterprise is integrating multiple sales force automation (SFA) and CRM solutions using an AI tool to get a stronger view of the customer and sales pipeline.

Company Context

UandMe is a company operating globally with offices in the US, Mexico, UK, Germany, Australia and Japan.

The Business Challenge

The company is highly acquisitive and over the last five years has ended up with two instances of Salesforce, an instance each of Microsoft Dynamics, Hubspot and Oracle. They are undergoing consolidation as a business to remove overlaps and duplication and drive for an improvement to how they manage all important interactions with customers. Crucially, as part of preparing for IPO in 2025, there is a significant need for more accurate and insightful sales pipeline and revenue forecasting, and a strong need for improvement in customer support.

The Existing Challenges

Multiple SFA and CRM solutions are in active use leading to data silos and hindered central visibility of information.

With different sales processes configured in these systems, there are challenges in getting a holistic view of sales pipeline and revenue forecasts.

Important customer support processes need improvement to drive better operational metrics and increase customer satisfaction.

The Proposed Solution Incorporating AI

The chief architect has recommended that the business purchase and deploy an AI-enabled unified intelligence engine instead of an alternative proposal to transform and migrate all of these instances of CRM and SFA tools into one single instance. The benefit to this approach, she argues, is that the business processes that are active in each operating company can remain for the most part in the short- to medium-term. This serves to reduce large-scale disruption and avoids ripping out existing systems, which is a key concern with sales and support leadership. By using an AI engine to consolidate and enrich the data, the project team will get early insight into where there is misalignment or gaps in the business processes and will be able to reflect this and set out a rapid roadmap of process change to fulfill the reporting and intelligence requirements.

Components of the Solution (see figure 17)

System connectors
Robust standard integrations which can be switched on to facilitate rapid data extraction from existing systems

Intelligent integration processors
Modules which have been designed for the domain-handling entities such as opportunities, customers and process stages and which include intelligent abilities to cleanse, transform, and prepare data for analysis

Reference data models
Standard master data entities which provide the foundation for reference across systems and ensure consistent data representation across the organization

In-house and third-party AI models
A suite of machine learning models which can be selected to analyze data to identify patterns, trends and anomalies. Models can be fine-tuned on corporate data context to increase accuracy and precision

Insight and Inference
Analysis and generation capabilities which carry out some data transformation, processing and generate actionable insights and recommendations

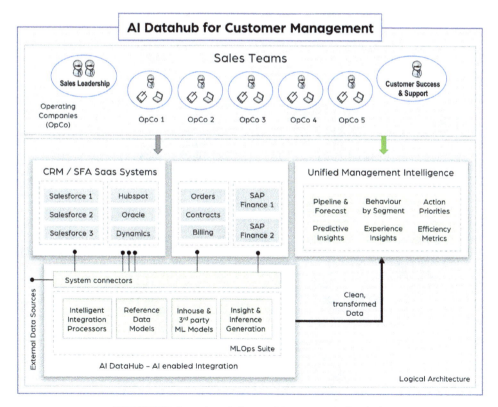

FIGURE 17. *Sample solution architecture—AI datahub.*

This AI-powered approach changes the game for enterprise integration.

A) Data integration methodologies

We will see a shift from traditional methods involving ETL or EAI platforms interfacing with individual systems, leading to a complex set of connections that are difficult to maintain and scale. The AI-first solution proposes using pre-built connectors and intelligent processors to extract, transform and load data from various sources into a central repository. Using machine learning opens the path to automatically identify and address data inconsistencies, missing values and duplicates. This can help improve accuracy at source and facilitates a potential master data management (MDM) layer, a single source of truth for customer, product or offer catalog and other critical information. This solution can also facilitate real-time data integration using APIs, enabling faster access to insights and allowing businesses to react to changes in real time.

B) Platform consolidation and digital transformation

The proposed solution will enable the operating companies to leverage their existing CRM and SFA systems without the need for a complete migration. This minimizes disruption to ongoing operations and avoids the high costs associated with replacing established platforms. The second benefit is through identifying process misalignments and gaps. Joining the data paves the way for targeted process improvements. Each team can avoid the distraction of large-scale system change and focus on improving their workflows across sales, marketing and customer service. Platform consolidation can involve long implementation times. The proposed solution offers a faster path through enabling data integration and insights generation without requiring a complete system overhaul. This allows businesses to adapt more quickly to changing market dynamics and customer needs.

C) Principle of data first, process second, platform third

Data becomes the foundation. By prioritizing data and establishing a unified layer accessible across the various operating companies, this helps all applications and processes move towards consistent, high-quality data. This data-driven approach can further help by ensuring that process changes are targeted and address the most critical bottlenecks and inefficiencies. To me, it is so important that technology is an enabler, not a constraint. The proposed solution allows businesses to get more benefit from their existing platforms, eventually freeing them from vendor lock-in associated with specific CRM or SFA platforms, and promotes a more flexible approach to technology adoption.

D) Longer term roadmap to a central platform

The business can prioritize taking out or replacing the systems that impact the most over a longer period and get the best benefit or cost savings in the near term. Having a roadmap to a central platform offers a scalable solution that can accommodate future growth and changing business needs. As the organization expands further through organic growth or acquisition, the solution should be able to adapt and integrate new data sources seamlessly. The AI suite can relatively quickly become the central hub for data analysis and insights. This should reduce or even eliminate the need for duplication across reporting tools and enables consistent, data-driven decision-making.

Risks and Challenges

As part of the case study, it is important to recognize that the approach is not without some risks and challenges, such as:

Implementing and maintaining an effective AI solution requires access to skilled professionals with expertise in data science and machine learning.

Centralizing customer and commercial data like this at scale needs strong security measures to protect sensitive information and compliance with data privacy regulations.

There may be teams that are resistant to change if they see this platform as a threat. Their early involvement and inclusion will be key to success.

The Next Phase

Looking out to a longer-term horizon, it is possible to imagine several scenarios that AI will develop towards. One of them involves improvements to large language models (LLMs). As you would expect with the market forces behind AI at this time, the number of research initiatives and developments in this space are unbelievably numerous and becoming hard to track! There are many useful sources such as The Neuron, a daily email newsletter, and Lex Fridman's podcasts. I've zoomed in and picked out these areas to examine in the LLM space:

1. Self-Refine

This is a proposed architecture where the initial response generated is then processed (by the same LLM) to provide feedback on the output. The same LLM then uses this feedback to refine the answer. This process is repeated either for a specified number of iterations or until the model determines that no further refinement is necessary. Instead of providing straight, one-shot answers, the idea is that LLMs would become capable of self-refinement and continuous improvement. The goal is to boost accuracy, clarity and the overall quality of the response.

2. Chain of Thought

This research shows that reasoning abilities emerge naturally in large language models when a simple method called chain-of-thought prompting is used. This is where some chain-of-thought demonstrations are provided as examples within the prompt. By providing smaller worked examples like the main question within the prompt, the research team has shown it can improve LLM performance on a range of arithmetic, commonsense and symbolic reasoning tasks. This shows promise for LLMs tackling more complex tasks requiring multi-step logic and problem-solving.

3. Reflection

This research proposes a modular approach, and it uses three distinct models:

- the actor, an LLM that generates text and actions
- an evaluator that scores the outputs
- a self-reflection model (adapted from the self-refine idea above)

There are also short-term and long-term memory components which are an important part of the architecture. The actor will condition decisions and output based on short- and long-term memory, similar to the way humans remember recent events while also recalling important experiences from long-term memory. The actor, evaluator and self-reflection models will work through trials together in a loop, until the evaluator deems the response to be sufficient. In some cases, the reflection architecture has proven to improve performance in the experimental tasks by 20 percent. These ideas are prime examples of ways that LLM architecture will evolve and improve over the coming years.

Beyond NLP—Natural Language Understanding

Natural language processing encompasses all the capabilities we explored in chapter 3: neural networks, transformer models, LLMs and the ability of machine learning models to learn the logical associations between words and phrases. This learned structure of grammar and language is used to make predictions from inputs and generate realistic responses when asked questions. Natural language understanding (NLU) will go beyond syntax, diving into semantics to capture the intent behind the words and phrases. NLU systems will consider the broader context to infer meaning and intent when assessing questions and generating responses. NLU will likely have to use some advanced reasoning capabilities and mimic a human-like commonsense approach to make logical inferences and understand nuances in language. There are some experts who argue that LLMs will not be able to develop or incorporate this type of reasoning ability and are looking to new emerging models such as joint embedding architecture (JEDA). Yann Lecun of Meta AI is one expert who is a fan of this architecture and believes it will replace or supersede the transformer model in time.

Let is re-visit the comparison between LLMs to preschooler-learning ability again. We will see the technology breakthrough beyond Level 5 and into Level 6-type reasoning ability. The emerging ML models will be able to simulate thoughts about language itself, and be able to discuss grammar rules, word meanings and language structure. At Level 6, the model should also be able to use language effectively in a social context. It would simulate an understanding of behavioral cues by taking turns in conversations and use language to achieve limited goals in communication with a human. NLU algorithms and models are being considered as I write this, though no commercial announcements have been made public yet.

Data-Driven Modeling

This can be simply described as creating software out of data. The concept is that a team would start out with a dataset and use machine learning to extract knowledge from the data. This will evolve quickly into the process of using the data along with prompts and copilots to rapidly design and write software for almost any business purpose. When there is a lot of data, machine learning algorithms can do far better than humans at understanding and processing it. The same will eventually apply to the software we write.

New Types of Perceptrons in Neural Networks

The human brain has evolved over millions of years and as we advance towards AGI, we will further leverage how it works in the software we create. This would mean we have to design next-generation neurons (perceptrons) which include more of the deeper functions of human cells in the neural network models that we use in machine learning. There are three main types of neurons in our nervous system:

- Motor neurons control our body movements by transmitting electrical impulses to our muscles. Software that controls any kind of device for kinetic movement could choose to model these more closely.

- Sensory neurons help us feel sensation. If you stub your toe, sensory neurons will send chemical and electrical impulses through the nervous system to let your brain know that you feel pain in your toe. An AI system could mimic how humans learn and adapt from rich sensory feedback and include this capability in machine learning models.

- Interneurons are the nerve cells that connect the motor and sensory neurons to each other. There could be opportunities to understand what roles these play in transmitting information to the brain. For instance, do they augment signals or add information in any way? This understanding could be useful when designing the next generation of machine learning models.

There are also other features of neurons that we could examine as candidates for including in machine learning model design. Human neurons contain dendrites, which look like tree branches that collect information to bring back to the neuron. At the end of the dendrite is a contact point called a synapse. A neuron can have just a few connections, or it can have sometimes hundreds of thousands of synaptic connections with itself, neighboring neurons or neurons in other regions of the brain. The synapse also serves as a junction where both the transmission and processing of information occur. We know that synapses are formed and eliminated daily in our nervous systems, but they are black boxes, researchers have not yet discovered what happens in the neuron during this process. Machine learning models are largely static in terms of the connections that are present. It is not hard to imagine that sometime in the near future, these software models will become more organic in nature and have the ability to build new connections based on learning, some level of reasoning and perhaps even response to stimulus.

Event Processing Crossed with Machine Learning

The field of complex event processing (CEP) and event-driven architecture has some crossover with AI, and I propose that this connection could be further strengthened. We see CEP in use today in areas like fraud detection, business activity monitoring, customer experience management and Internet of Things applications. CEP principles enable solution designers to build software to extract meaning from lots of different data streams. In the real world, events will happen at different levels of abstraction and at different times. When we have multiple sources of events at different levels, it is known as an "event cloud."

Example scenario: A financial services company uses a CEP solution to monitor transactions for signs of fraudulent activity. The tool would continuously analyze these streams of data:

- raw transactions (type, amount, location, time)

- customer information (past transactions, account history)

- external data sources (watchlists from authorities, blocked cards)

The solution would be configured to recognize patterns of events that might indicate potential fraud, such as multiple purchase attempts from different geographical locations or a large purchase at an unusual time. When this suspicious pattern is detected the CEP system can trigger actions like blocking the transaction, alerting the internal fraud team for further investigation and notifying the merchant and the customer verification. CEP applies domain knowledge across multiple data sources to understand what is happening in terms of high-level concepts and complex events. If we combine the power of CEP and event-driven architecture with AI and machine learning techniques, this could include events streaming into a ML model which could offer the following possibilities:

- adaptive automation where the AI components learn and help inform the next action to be taken based on real-time events, leading to more effective and dynamic products and platforms

- disciplines of machine learning combined to provide explainable insights behind the detected patterns and triggered actions

- solution possibly designed to automate the model selection and even hyperparameter tuning based on the type of data encountered in real time

- product prices adjusted in real time based on demand, competitor analysis and customer sentiment

- AI models leveraged to predict future events based on incoming CEP data streams

Increasing Number of Black Box Components

As machine learning models advance in scale, we will see software solutions that operate like a black box, where the designers and owners will not be able to fully explain how they work. This is already true of some of the large language models at the lowest level of behavior, and I see this trend of increasing complexity continuing. It currently takes between seven and ten years to become a registered medical practitioner and that is without a specialization. I can see a time coming very soon where high-end software design incorporating advanced AI techniques will be as complex as some medical disciplines. The opposite impact on medical professionals is very likely where Machine Learning tools could reduce the amount of time it takes to become a radiographer or specialist. We can see a path to where machine learning can offer powers of diagnosis and disease detection way beyond human capabilities. AI technology has the potential to reduce human suffering in the world. It comes down to a matter of choice. Where will the money for investments flow? What will our priorities look like in the new software and AI technology landscape?

Increasingly Hybrid Architectures

Software will be designed to make real-time decisions based on data that streams through the system. Software design will embrace dynamic, almost fluid rulesets that act in the interests of a range of goals such as speed, accuracy or safety. These objectives, supported with machine learning capabilities, will mean software implementations that will become much more complex than the traditional workflow or task-driven systems that we currently use. It should be possible to toggle these objectives within a well-architected system. For example, in times of peak demand, accuracy could be reduced in favor of speed of response. Another alternative is where safety of the outcome—no errors can be tolerated—is the primary objective, therefore the speed of response has to be secondary. I do see a return to the craft of intelligent software design as becoming part of the competitive DNA of a modern business. It seems to me that the abstraction of complexity and availability of services and infrastructure has made a lot of software look and behave the same.

The journey that we are on in this new era is already fascinating. We will see the disciplines merge and design patterns transfer between traditional software and AI domains. Fast forward three to five years and we may not even be talking about AI anymore. We will also very likely not be talking about software as we do today. We will be using phrases like models, agents, prompts, learning and safety much more in our everyday discussions. I see this becoming like a giant game of PAC-MAN. As the "software-PAC" continues to eat the world, there is a bigger, better, faster "AI-PAC" chasing it down. This AI-PAC will be different, though. Instead of simply eating software, it will leave behind new and more interesting creations. As a metaphor, we are hoping that while AI will be a disruptive force, it will be a net contributor to the universe. It will help us generate, validate and curate software on a scale and to a level of quality that we as humans would struggle to achieve alone.

The Impact on People Connected to Software

"As we integrate AI into our lives, we must never forget the importance of human connection, empathy, and compassion."

—RANA EL KALIOUBY

We can examine the impact of AI on the people connected to software from two points of view: those who work directly in software development and almost everyone else who works in business today! These perspectives will offer some answers to the key question: what does the future hold?

You may not work directly in software development, but you still need to care about AI. You are likely part of a business / operational team who uses software every day. Much of what this community presently knows about AI will be driven by mainstream media. With the widespread coverage given to generative AI in the last while, we can safely say this has had a profound impact. Attention-grabbing headlines proclaim that AI is going to take away all our jobs. From research and discussions with various people in this segment, the feedback is that if complex jobs like software development are at risk, then what hope do people in routine operational roles have? I want to offer the following perspective. Think about where the risks are. The first risk with people in this group is if they don't take the time to truly understand what the AI capabilities offer and how they are progressing. The impact here is they will not be prepared when change comes to their role or business function and then are seen as lacking relevant skills to embrace the inevitable AI advance. The second is where decision-makers buy into the marketing hype without fully probing for specific and longer-term implications of purchase decisions. Jumping into a quick adoption of a new AI toolset that suddenly becomes obsolete or poses a security risk would be a terrible decision. To be fair, many organizations will find it incredibly difficult to choose a single AI platform to replace existing applications for business use. The capabilities are evolving too fast right now.

The third risk in assessing AI from outside the software domain is where executives set ambitious goals for AI adoption based on financial metrics alone. It is not hard to imagine the impact here: drive efficiency at all costs and remove the expensive human employees! Bring in the AI tools to increase margin and profit! There are enormous risks in this approach. Employees will likely see these trends ahead of time and begin to leave industries or professions where AI replacement becomes a pattern. The knock-on impact could be a premature loss of skills and domain knowledge with the resulting gaps biting into customer experience and customer retention. Such a scenario would then actually subvert the original goal of margin growth and leave the organization vulnerable.

What's the Right Path to Follow?

For people in this group, closely connected to technology and who are not software professionals, I recommend the following:

A) Develop a good understanding of the basic technical fundamentals of AI machine learning. This will involve some investment of your personal time outside of work, but it will prove vital.

B) Interact with product teams to get a handle on the definitions of AI for your business. This means discussing and agreeing on:

- where we are with AI

- what AI tools and technologies are being considered

- What are the objectives for the next eighteen months, the next three years

- What benefits are we are looking to achieve for our customers, our internal processes and for our employees

C) Volunteer for a side project to gain hands-on experience with AI tools, either a formal project in the workplace or on your own time. This wave is too important to sit on the sidelines and be a spectator! There are many ways to do this:

- Play around with prompts and carry out some quick "prompt engineering" on the freely available chatbots.

- Use generative AI as part of your workweek. It can help you plan, create meeting minutes, generate content like business process documentation.

- Offer to act as a subject matter expert and help with AI model testing.

- Offer to assist with data preparation or data cleaning to play a part in the machine learning pipeline.

AI will cause this group both fear and excitement. Fear of the disruption AI will bring, and excitement at its potential opportunities.

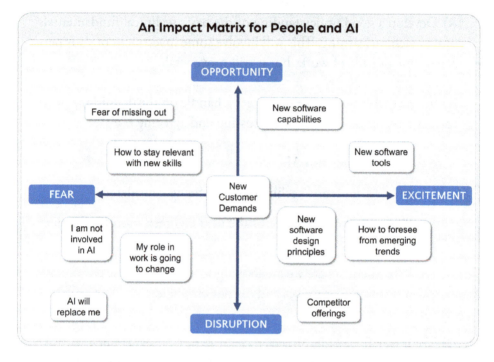

FIGURE 18. *An impact matrix.*

It is important to consider some of the potential negative consequences that may directly affect people, so let's explore the fear and disruption side of the matrix.

I Am Not Involved

This new wave will create two groups—those who have and those who have not—just like any other wave of technology change in the past. It is already happening in many businesses where the AI innovators are forging ahead and getting to grips with the technology, learning about the risks and spotting opportunities before everyone else. The same insights we offered to nonprofessionals fully apply here! Do not sit on the sidelines. Develop an understanding and acquire some AI skills as soon as you possibly can.

My Role is Going to Change

This is a fact of life for everyone involved in software. We look at this in more detail in the next section.

AI Will Replace Me

One of the biggest fears is that AI will cause widespread job losses across various industries. As tasks are automated at scale, the concern is that certain roles will become obsolete, resulting in unemployment and economic disruption. It seems likely that many roles in the software industry can be replaced and human expertise largely bypassed. An AI-powered software tool that costs $20 a month on subscription could be used to replace a human being engaged part time for $2,000. What is the long-term impact of this type of creative economic destruction? Skills are commoditized and human expertise is considered less valuable. Companies can make staff with these skills redundant to reduce cost. Certain consulting and freelance businesses fail as work dries up. There is less incentive for young people to enter the profession. In a worst-case scenario, the skill base becomes further commoditized and the expertise eventually becomes quite scarce and artisan. There is an arc forming that suggests that the jobs of graphic designer, software tester and technical writer will be the first to succumb.

There is hope, however, where the value offered by human workers is too complex and nuanced that AI will not be able to readily replace. Consider a practitioner offering a deep consultation providing multiple ideas and options based on the wider business context. Humans can pick up on body language and emotional tones. They can form relationships with their team and customers that can never be replaced by a machine. Professionals relating their direct experience of failure and lessons learned from previous projects? These are real visceral experiences that senior people will refer to as the key career learning points, which helped avoid repeats of past mistakes. Picture a multimedia presentation of a consultant providing explanations face-to-face on the options that were considered for a project brief, with pros and cons explained on each of the choices made and why the final proposal was ultimately selected. These are all examples of humans in the real world offering significant value beyond the outcome of the task itself.

The power of teams of people from different disciplines collaborating in a room around a white board could not be replicated by AI in any foreseeable future scenario. How would AI replace the alignment, focus and follow through required to progress concepts from the workshop into the execution phase? It is almost always part of the evolution of a project that a change or tweak to a solution is required, and that is also best suited to human expertise.

We may see an emergence of guilds, unions or representative bodies that lobby governments and large corporate organizations to pledge support for professional workers. We have seen this happen recently with the writers' strike in Hollywood which was originally initiated to protect against the use of mini-rooms. These mini-rooms are basically workshops where writers are paid for their time on an hourly basis to come up with ideas and sketch out a plot for a movie or TV series. There is no long-term commitment and the ideas generated are owned by the studio. Suddenly, it was possible for the studios to take a generative AI tool, use these ideas and ask it to write detailed storyboards and full screenplays.

The Writers Guild of America went on strike for 146 days until a deal was reached on September 24, 2023. Under the terms of the deal, AI cannot be used to write or rewrite literary material and AI-generated content cannot be considered source material. What is also interesting is that writers are free to use AI to write scripts if they wish, but studios cannot force them to. This effectively puts the use of AI for scriptwriting under the control of writers instead of the studios and producers.

On the positive side, there will be plenty of opportunities and new jobs will be created that we haven't thought of yet. Some examples of roles that have exploded in the corporate world in the last ten years:

- customer success manager for SaaS companies

- content creators for social media advertising

- digital marketing specialist for promotion on the web

- cyber security analyst to protect against cyberattacks

If you have worked in technology for any amount of time, you have been through a fair share of hype cycles. Even those relatively new to the profession will have noticed the next big thing can be rapidly replaced with something fresh if it doesn't gain traction in the market. The metaverse and virtual reality is probably the most recent example, with Facebook pivoting into Meta and investing over thirty billion dollars in a new ecosystem they believe is a large part of the future of technology. Investors are wary of this and are not seeing signs of mass adoption. Still, Apple has also invested and released their latest VisionPro product, so there may be some life left in this one yet. AI is a different beast, though. It is no gimmick. The opportunities and disruptions for those involved will be quite significant.

The Impact of AI on Software Teams

We show an example structure of a modern software team in figure 19. The core roles are grouped at the top and the specialist roles at the bottom. Depending on the size of your organization, there will be various flavors of team structure assembled to tackle different phases of product delivery and types of projects. It is impossible to cover all scenarios/industries in this book, so what we discuss here is a typical team involved in developing tools for business use. We don't cover the more specific specialist roles involved in areas such as pure infrastructure tooling, mobile app development, telecoms, utilities or manufacturing, however, the general principles remain the same. The most common AI roles are shown in green in figure 19 to help highlight where skills can be embedded within the team.

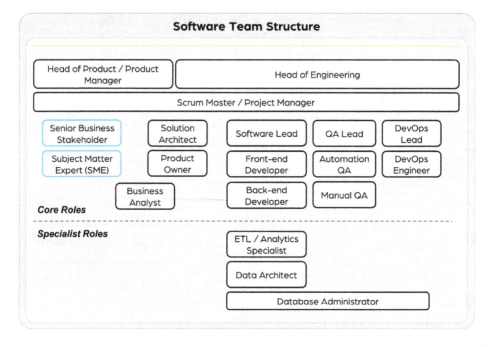

FIGURE 19. *Software team structure.*

As AI becomes a more important part of the software stack, there will be changes to traditional roles. Some will merge together and become hybrid roles. Brand new roles will emerge, too.

The Product Management Team

Artificial Intelligence is about to alter the rules of time and space when it comes to planning features, creating coherent roadmap release schedules and evolving the application or platform in response to competitive action and customer needs.

Figure 20 shows an outline of the important impacts across critical components of the process for the entire product management team.

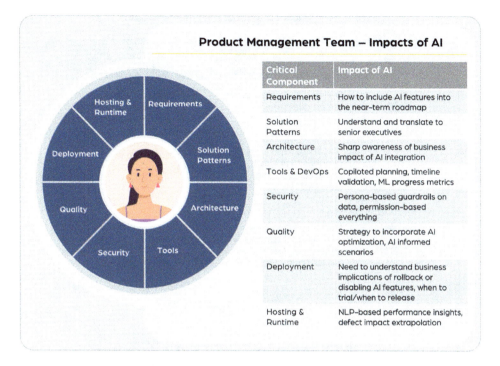

Product Management Team – Impacts of AI

Critical Component	Impact of AI
Requirements	How to include AI features into the near-term roadmap
Solution Patterns	Understand and translate to senior executives
Architecture	Sharp awareness of business impact of AI integration
Tools & DevOps	Copiloted planning, timeline validation, ML progress metrics
Security	Persona-based guardrails on data, permission-based everything
Quality	Strategy to incorporate AI optimization, AI informed scenarios
Deployment	Need to understand business implications of rollback or disabling AI features, when to trial/when to release
Hosting & Runtime	NLP-based performance insights, defect impact extrapolation

FIGURE 20. *Product management team—impacts of AI.*

Let's examine the impact on the most common job titles that are used in the product management discipline or "job family." The following table holds a summary of the roles featured in this section. We include the data scientist in this section as we believe this role will have more of a business orientation as AI becomes more important in the software stack. This role has been propelled to the front of the stage and is increasingly facing off to business stakeholders for important aspects of the overall software solution.

TABLE 7 – Impacts on product management teams

Role and Seniority	Primary Responsibility and Focus	Impact of AI
Product Manager Senior to VP level	Defining and delivering on the product's vision and strategy	Pressure from stakeholders to make informed decisions about how to incorporate AI into the product/platform. Will have to balance commitments made to the C suite with what is possible in their product teams.
	Managing the team and priorities to achieve roadmap goals and outcomes	
Scrum Master Mid-level to senior	Facilitate the software development team to deliver projects on time and within forecasted budgets	The core role of a scrum master is to address risks and remove blockers. This role will need to be educated to be able to spot and manage the new risks and blockers that AI capabilities will bring.
	Sprint planning, daily standups, sprint reviews and retrospectives.	
Product Owner Mid-level to senior	Delivering and aligning product capabilities with the needs of the business.	Lack of AI expertise will hold back progression of people in this role over the medium term. Will need to embrace the "try, test, fail, try again" approach that AI requires.
	Manage customer and operational engagement to drive launch of capabilities.	
Business Analyst Junior to mid-level	Understand business needs and translate them into requirements.	This role will quickly start to include aspects of data science and awareness of machine learning techniques. Will need to be comfortable in defining success metrics for AI capabilities in business terms.
	Maintain a coherent and actionable pipeline of prioritized business needs.	
Data Scientist Mid-level to senior	Identifies metrics and opportunities for improving business processes, products and services.	The team will rely on this AI role to share disciplines. Key skills for success will be the ability to mentor and explain techniques well. Will lead in the management of data and choices of ML models, contributing strongly to the delivery of the overall business solution.
	Performs data mining, exploration and analysis. Designs, trains and implements machine learning models.	

The Product Manager

Many senior product managers in our industry today are overwhelmed with broad areas of responsibility. An important portion of their time goes into managing upwards. Their set of stakeholders range from senior business executives from sales and marketing with their go-to-market imperatives, CIO/risk managers with ongoing security concerns and gaps, and operations, to customer success and support teams with an endless supply of defects or feature tweaks (depending on your view). The product or platform roadmap can often get diluted with new directives that limit the amount of time they have for innovation.

Product managers will have to quickly become experts at both explaining the impacts of AI trends and new capabilities to senior executives, while also managing expectations on what is possible. They will have to keep informed on the latest innovations and grasp the impact or relevance for their business. They will be asked to provide sales and marketing teams with enough customer insight to allow for future product market positioning. Many modern technology businesses sell future features to their prospects and customers ahead of time. This is going to become even more relevant with AI, and a very big challenge for all members of the product management team. They will have to juggle commitments made internally and externally to the market while building new capabilities. As leaders in shaping the product and platform roadmap, there will be pressure on product managers/VP of product to provide a coherent strategy for the business and technical stakeholders in the organization. Successfully navigating this pressure will require preparation and discussion with solution architects, data science and machine learning domain experts to build a thoughtful and guided path for many teams to follow. It will be imperative to anticipate probable failures along the way and these will offer points of learning to everyone. Communicating this in advance will be critical to protect the confidence of senior sponsors in the team. The following are questions that people in this role should address as soon as possible:

- Where are the risks for competitive disruption to our business model?

- What are the best datasets that might be candidates for AI solutions?

- Should we plan for AI capabilities above the line and below the line?

- What AI objectives can be set for six, twelve and eighteen months from now?

- What would an AI ecosystem look like for us three years from now?

The Scrum Master

The scrum master is the heartbeat of the software creation process as they identify and remove roadblocks to keep the team moving forward. They champion Agile values, ensuring everyone works in sync with the chosen methodology. Their toolkit often includes daily stand-ups, sprint planning and retrospectives, and they focus on team engagement and timely, on-budget project delivery. As AI changes the software landscape, the scrum master must evolve, too. They'll need to manage the unique challenges of machine learning pipelines, perhaps working data scientists and ML engineers. We dive into machine learning operations (MLOps) in chapter 5 and explore how AI will transform the development process there.

How will the scrum master adapt to the impact of AI? There are many crossovers with the business analyst, including continuous learning and building relationships with the data science and machine learning team members. I also advise scrum masters to:

- Bring experimentation into sprints. Model development involves some degree of experimentation. Scrum masters should be prepared to adjust sprint structures and expectations to accommodate this process, balancing agility with the need for strong model validation.

- Facilitate AI-augmented workflows. Scrum masters can identify areas where AI tools can streamline or automate tasks within the development process (e.g., code generation, automated testing, intelligent task prioritization). This requires understanding AI capabilities and collaborating with the team to implement these tools effectively.

The Product Owner

The product owner will represent the operational stakeholders when the team moves deeper into the implementation work. They hold responsibility for providing solutions to support a scalable, digital journey and workflow. These workflows must be sharp and efficient for customers, suppliers and internal staff to achieve profitable business outcomes. They should aim for constant alignment with SMEs and end users in understanding all functional and non-functional needs from the product/platform. These needs will cover important areas like automation, efficiency and a strong user experience.

Product owners will have to become significantly more connected to how AI will influence the direct outcomes of the software creation process. They can achieve this by leaning into the AI team and actively collaborating with the AI technical lead, the data scientist and machine learning implementation engineers throughout the development process and aiming to build a confident understanding of the end-to-end machine learning pipeline. This will be especially important in the early projects, so I recommend the product owner starts discussing project goals, how datasets are selected, how models are trained and how to mitigate challenges like potential biases. It will be important to proactively participate in testing and evaluating the effectiveness of AI solutions. They should eventually play a key role in identifying potential issues, and ensure any solution aligns with user needs and business goals. Product owners are usually metric driven, so the ability to measure and reflect success or deviations for new AI features will be vital. In presenting clear and transparent metrics, this can help demonstrate the stages of the journey, and give confidence to senior management on progress. Finally, to offset any gaps in experience or knowledge in AI techniques, product owners should attend relevant conferences and webinars and meet regularly with people who are going through the same journey.

The Business Analyst

The business analyst is a traditional role in software development and one which is going to change significantly as AI becomes a wider part of the solution options. The business analyst has direct responsibility for identifying and performing the correct level of analysis to shape requirements and process definitions for an effective solution. The requirements and solution needs should be expressed in terms that support both the external customer journey and the internal business teams in managing workflow processes efficiently. They are detail-oriented and are typically heavily involved in the creation of:

- data flow diagrams
- business rules
- dependency map and traceability matrix
- test approach, and often the test plan

A business analyst will set out standards for a strong set of documented standard procedures that the operational business user community can then maintain. They should aim to provide output and collateral that helps inform all members of the delivery team, especially more technical staff to bring business orientation and alignment. As AI features and capabilities become more of a part of the overall software stack, I believe the role of business analyst will have to overlap and collaborate heavily with the data scientist and machine learning specialists. There are some who think the complete separation of business and technical disciplines is positive, but I tend to disagree. The best analysts I have worked with have hybrid skills and a working knowledge of the design patterns and technology stack capabilities. We are just talking about product screens, platform workflows and configuration settings. This should be considered table stakes as part of the work domain. What I am referring to is knowledge of the components of the architecture, what APIs are important, and how data is served to users and managed in the system. As AI components are developed and integrated, the business analyst should aim to be confident and familiar with these and learn to envision how they can be used and how they will evolve. Business analysts are called to:

- Embrace the hybrid approach. Business analysts should develop a hybrid skill set that bridges the gap between business needs and technical capabilities. It will be critical to include a foundational understanding of AI and machine learning concepts.

- Go beyond the user interface. It is so important to go beyond the user interface and gain familiarity with the underlying architecture, APIs and AI data management practices.

- Build relationships with the AI technical lead, data scientists and machine learning specialists.

- Learn continuously about the evolving landscape of AI. Actively seek opportunities to build knowledge and skills.

The Data Scientist

As seen from the diagram, the rest of the team will rely on the data scientist to share their techniques and approaches. In many companies during the big data phase, data scientists used to work independently or with other data professionals, focusing on data analysis and reporting. This position has evolved rapidly. Now, collaboration is crucial, and the data scientist is expected to work with people from the business, product and technical domains.

TABLE 8 – The data scientist's role in the AI and machine learning lifecycle

Step	Description	Data Scientist Role
Business problem definition	Understand the business problem and translate it into a machine learning problem.	Work with the SME, the business analyst and product owner to understand the problem and desired outcomes. Lead the early discussions on metrics, data and machine learning solution options. Help identify and review potential data sources and their suitability for the chosen problem.
Data collection and preparation	Collect, clean and pre-process data for model training.	Organize and manage the pre-processing of data, e.g., by handling missing values, outliers and inconsistencies. Lead the feature engineering effort to create new features that improve model performance. Split the data into training and testing sets.
Model building, training and validation	Select, build, train and validate machine learning models.	Work with ML experts to choose the right machine learning algorithms based on the problem and data characteristics. Design and implement model architecture including hyperparameter tuning. Train the model and evaluate its performance using various metrics (e.g., accuracy, precision, recall). Refine the model as appropriate based on the evaluation results.
Model deployment and monitoring	Deploy the model to production and monitor its performance.	Work with the ML engineers and MLOps team to deploy the model into a production environment. Agree the process of monitoring performance in life and identify potential issues like performance degradation or data drift. Decide on retraining or redeploying the model when needed to maintain its effectiveness.

The data scientist is ultimately responsible for making sense of complex data, and figuring out how data can be used to generate valuable business insights and solve real world problems. One of the key skills to overall success in AI initiatives will be the ability of the data scientist to mentor other team members through the process and explain techniques to both business and technical team members.

Before the final summary in this section, we briefly highlight the domain orientation of the different roles that will participate in AI-related product initiatives. We present three lanes representing business, product and AI domains. The roles will sit in one or more of these lanes to indicate the emphasis of the activities and responsibilities. We include a short commentary on three of the roles.

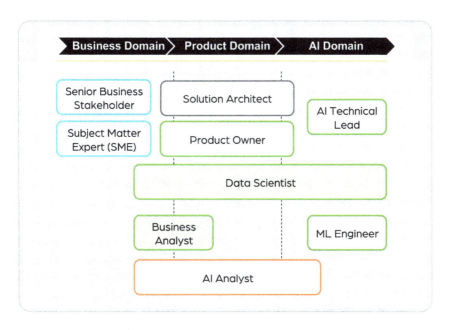

FIGURE 21. *Domain orientation.*

Senior Business Stakeholder

If the product team are champions of the AI initiative, then this role will need to be involved from the start to ensure they understand the reasons for making the investment. I would expect that senior business stakeholders will demand to be involved though, and we can expect them to initiate discussion about the opportunities for including an innovation in AI to support their teams.

Subject Matter Expert (SME)

This role is vital to help AI initiatives in many ways.

- Data collection and labeling: The SME can help identify relevant data sources for AI projects and participate in data collection efforts. Their understanding of specific tasks and processes will enable them to label and annotate data correctly for training AI models.

- Voice of the user: The role of a SME can offer valuable insights into user behavior, expectations, hidden assumptions and common workarounds to problems. They can help through being involved in testing, providing feedback and participating in design workshops.

- Mitigating bias: Based on their understanding of common industry practice and experience as a super user, they can help identify potential biases as AI models are tested.

Subject matter experts should be involved heavily in the requirements, understanding and design activities of AI initiatives. Their colleagues should take time to share some high level technical knowledge with them to help them participate effectively.

AI Technical Lead

As AI initiatives become part of the broader software landscape, we are starting to see this job title emerge. LinkedIn searches indicate this is a role that is rapidly becoming popular, typically filled by someone coming from a machine learning or data science background who oversees the technical design and delivery of AI solutions. The key responsibilities indicate they work closely with the solution architect to ensure there is alignment with existing applications or platforms. The people in this role are likely to have a formal technical qualification and probably not a huge depth of business experience, so they will need coaching and support on the non-technical aspects of the role such as commercial matters or people management. The AI technical lead should:

- Look for commercial insight. Actively seek out guidance on commercial aspects of AI projects, stakeholder management and team leadership to complement technical skills.

- Prioritize explainability: Many people will be unsure or even skeptical when they first encounter AI models. It will be highly valuable to provide explanations into how machine learning models work, and this will foster trust and understanding between teams.

- Keep up to speed with MLOps. MLOps principles are moving fast. As technical lead it will be vital to stay on top of new tools, open-source solution options for model deployment, monitoring and continuous improvement across test, production and training environments.

- Focus on integration. Most people in this role will have to work into an existing platform or application. It will be important to develop an understanding of the existing systems and architectures to help bring decent integration of any AI solution components.

TABLE 9 – Summary of how AI will impact the product management team

Critical component	Impact of AI
Requirements creation	▪ The product management team will have to focus more on their knowledge of business data. They will need to know principles of data science and the basic mechanics of machine learning to identify opportunities to add intelligence to the application or platform. ▪ AI will create fresh user engagement channels (conversational UI, virtual assistants, chatBots). ▪ The team will need knowledge of how to incorporate and integrate these capabilities using APIs and data. ▪ They will need to be able to write requirements from the perspective of customer personas and for internal users to get full business value from the new capabilities. ▪ They will need expertise in preparing the business for launching new channels and adapting to AI capabilities as they drop.
Solution patterns	▪ This team will be pushed to oversee requirements that are coherent and aligned to machine learning, e.g., predictive or generative models. ▪ They will have to come up with stronger design validation principles and refine their models for business value estimation to include metrics and success and failure criteria. ▪ Business logic in the application will gain strength as the workflow will be able to learn, e.g., identify and remove exceptions from the task flow, intercepting additional manual tasks as the capability allows. This will stretch how product owners, business analysts and solution architects think about software today.
Software Architecture	▪ When carrying out roadmap planning, good business awareness of AI tools and capabilities will be key; it will no longer be the sole preserve of technical teams, solution or DevOps architects. ▪ The product manager, owner and BA will need to think deeply about their existing applications and look for opportunities to integrate with (potentially multiple) AI services. ▪ Different types of services will evolve as machine learning components allow applications to learn from user behavior. This will evolve further as the ability of the software to intercept manual tasks and protect users against data breaches and repeated process failures.

Critical component	Impact of AI
Security	▪ Product Management teams will need proper guardrails on how to control and consume data and should not have to build or design this separately. ▪ They should receive security as a service to facilitate "permission-based everything" for all key dependencies to the software process, e.g., correct access to environments, regular automated user attestation for applications and data privacy controls. ▪ We will see deeper oversight from regulatory bodies holding teams accountable for transparency in design decisions and in runtime behavior of data in the application.
Quality	▪ Generative AI will be used extensively to write informed test scenarios and plans for all software components, with full insight into test coverage and negative testing. ▪ Product management teams will be able to move far beyond A/B testing, towards built-in AI optimization which could augment and improve the application on the fly as it learns from certain control conditions and parameters. ▪ It is likely that AI-powered QA automation tools will be able to consume APIs and application interfaces at all levels of the stack. As part of the execution and reporting on test scenarios, this will feed into the ability for the product/platform to continuously adapt and improve the coverage and level of testing.
Deployment and DevOps	▪ Product management teams will not be directly served with enhancements or impacts here. They will benefit from much stronger insights and service provided by other roles, in particular the DevOps architect who will be able to model out various scenarios of deployment to aid in release planning and overall cost management.
Hosting and Runtime	▪ Technically advanced product management teams will be able to look for performance feedback and insights into machine learning and AI components of their product/platform. ▪ They will start to measure software defect impacts and carry out defect impact extrapolation—a term not widely used but introduced here. This is largely manual and subjective today. It will become much more powerful, with AI capabilities seeking to measure downtime, intervention time, workaround time and inform self-healing prioritization. This will appear in both public cloud IaaS platforms (e.g., AWS Cloudwatch) and bespoke software.

continued ▶

Critical component	Impact of AI

Adoption and use	• As AI tools become commoditized and widespread, pressure will appear from two directions:
	  – Competitors and startups will launch features extremely rapidly.
	  – End users will be expected to adopt new features faster.
	
	This will place huge pressure on planning and training times for product owners.

Ongoing maintenance	• Product management teams will have solutions for measuring risk from within the application itself. These will cover some important risks such as security, including risk of data being leaked, risk of intrusion, risk of downtime from releases/changes/defects or infrastructure failure, and risk of low ROI through measuring active use of features and specific scenarios.

The Software Development and Testing Team

The figure below highlights the key impact themes for the software development team. It is obvious to say AI tools will improve automation of repetitive tasks and will be able to auto-generate code and software scaffolding which will help make software developers and test engineers more productive in terms of their output. That is only one aspect, however. The disciplines involved in thoughtful design and creating adaptable, resilient architectures that stand the test of time will remain a skill set in demand for the foreseeable future.

Figure 22 includes some summary points to consider how AI will impact each stage of the process. I recommend that people in the senior roles, especially the architects and software leads, quickly acquire familiarity in machine learning techniques and understand the delivery pipeline. They should also choose some specific and appropriate aspects of machine learning and data science and learn deeper skills in this area. One suggestion would be to identify some candidate solutions or design patterns that make sense to add to their platform/application. Another is to quickly try some early experiments in adding these to the stack. Some are likely to fail early on, but this is a vital part of the process of incorporating AI tools. As John C. Maxwell says, "Fail early, fail often, but always fail forward."

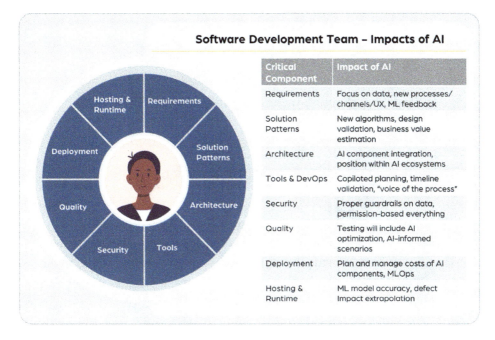

FIGURE 22. *Software development team impacts.*

Let's now examine each role in the software development team to get a better understanding of the potential impacts of AI.

Software/Solution Architect

The role of the solution architect is key in most software teams. They are responsible for defining and communicating a shared functional and technical architectural vision to ensure the solution is fit for purpose over a considerable time frame, usually three to five years. The architect must make decisions on solution patterns, the application or platform architecture and the choice of software components that will integrate together to form the overall solution. They should aim for the best long-term fit for the business to achieve measurable economic value.

Architects are going to have to adapt their thinking about design and architecture to incorporate AI tools into their platforms and applications. No strangers to change, software architects have had to adapt to cloud-based architectures as a frame of reference. These have evolved significantly since the launch of AWS EC2 in 2006 and Azure in 2010.

What we see as the major challenges with AI are:

- new applications/platform architectures emerging quickly

- many application features expected to be self-improving

- choosing the right AI tools, models, components

Software architects now have the task of constantly scanning the market to keep up to date with weekly or even daily market releases. AI will provide opportunities for experimentation and innovation, so architects will be in a key position to champion a culture of openness to explore how it can offer benefits to the entire process. This might not be easy with a team already under pressure, so offering timeouts or downtime between software releases will help. They allow team members to run mini projects on machine learning to try out new components and features for working objectives. Again, we come back to the "fail fast" principle that will be vital to encourage fresh thinking and stimulate ideas to make best use of the coming AI wave. Key calls to action for software architects:

- Shift more towards experimentation. Early AI initiatives often need to be prototyped and tested to find the solutions that best address business needs.

- Protect sensitive data and mitigate potential security vulnerabilities. Security best practices are required throughout the AI development lifecycle.

- Focus on adaptability and evolution as a design principle. Architects should consider factors like model explainability and using a modular architecture for future updates and troubleshooting.

- Proactively identify and mitigate bias in any machine learning models. This could be a blind spot for many architects—they will have to build skills and abilities in this area to ensure AI systems are fair, unbiased and non-discriminatory.

Software Technical Lead

The software technical lead is responsible for managing the software development team and supporting them in delivering high-quality software. Their work involves mentoring and managing software developers, aligning with other members of the delivery team to achieve overall objectives and assessing and measuring metrics that give feedback on software delivery progress and quality. They should aim to have a complete framework defined to cover use of development tools, code management practices, code review, test strategies and continuous integration/continuous deployment models. In response to the rise of AI, the software technical lead will need to develop new skills in areas like data analysis, machine learning and MLOps. Understanding the capabilities and the limitations of AI tools will help them collaborate with the AI specialists, but also challenge the appropriate and responsible use of these in the software development processes. There will be a balance to strike in delegating control of some implementation decisions, but also retaining a stake in overseeing quality and outcomes.

We have explored how there will be growing pressure to demonstrate the use of AI to keep pace with the times. In my experience, decisions taken at this level around specific implementation questions can massively influence the success of the overall solution. Consider that technical leads will tend to have limited time to achieve deadlines. It is a fact of life that they will have a slight bias towards technology familiar to them. Combine these factors with the possibility that AI vendors will make certain solutions convenient. So, it will be vital for the entire team to consider the implementation choices that are available and look longer-term beyond tight deadlines and convenience as reasons for selecting tools, components or vendor options. The software that technical leads implement will typically persist as containerized solutions for extended periods of time. If the solution functions reliably at scale, there will be little incentive to replace it. In this phase of AI, with machine learning tool sets, we will also see vendors and design patterns being rapidly superseded. The technical lead will have to be super careful about how they integrate (or allow the integration of) machine learning components into the software architecture.

Calls to Action for Software Technical Leads Involved in AI Initiatives:

- Develop new skills in data analysis, machine learning and MLOps

- Collaborate effectively with AI specialists to understand AI capabilities and limitations

- Challenge the appropriateness and responsible use of AI in software development

- Strike a balance between delegating control and maintaining oversight of quality and outcomes

- Look beyond deadlines and short-term convenience when choosing AI tools and solutions

- Integrate machine learning components into the software architecture with careful consideration for future scalability and maintainability

Software Developer

Traditionally, software developers have had responsibility for the creation, testing, debugging and delivery of the code that provides the required functionality in the application or platform. They aim to deliver high quality software that contains as few defects as possible, that can ideally perform at scale and handle data securely in transit and at rest. They will work as part of a team, using programming languages relevant to the technical stack and IT infrastructure chosen for the business, and create software applications or components based on requirements.

AI is already disrupting this role. The changes are set to evolve significantly in the coming years and will bring myriad benefits. Developers currently spend much of their time debugging and refactoring code. We will see later in the build section in chapter 5, where AI tools offer potential liberation from some of these tasks. Software developers will become a leading group of innovators/AI collaborators. This means understanding the capabilities and limitations of AI tools and knowing how to leverage them in the development process. They will also be interpreters, working with the data science and machine learning teams to help explain complex technical concepts to product managers and business stakeholders. They will need to be able to help translate business needs into parameters that AI systems can address, a skill they have practiced and honed through their careers.

One challenge I see immediately is that staying current on announcements and what is being released will continue to be difficult. The AI landscape is evolving rapidly. In the four months I have been researching this book, the number of announcements and developments was almost overwhelming. Software developers will be asked to continuously learn about new models, platforms and best practices. They'll need to be proactive in identifying areas where AI can add value to existing features or unlock entirely new features within the software they build.

Data will become even more central. In the same way that infrastructure became really important in the shift to the cloud, AI software developers skilled in data preparation and understanding how to effectively train AI models will be in high demand. They will need to work closely with data scientists and ML engineers, building the infrastructure for AI integration and ensuring responsible use of data. As AI augments the development process, it's crucial for software developers to embrace experimentation, iteration and a "fail fast" mentality. AI might not always provide perfect solutions on the first try, and debugging will involve understanding both the traditional codebase and the logic of the AI models.

Key Decisions for Software Developers to Make

- Skill development: Where should I invest time to build AI fluency (specific languages, frameworks, techniques)?

- Tool choice: Which AI platforms and libraries best align with our existing tech stack and future goals?

- Collaboration: How should we restructure teams and workflows to foster effective collaboration with data scientists and ML engineers?

- Testing and monitoring: What new approaches are needed to test and monitor software systems infused with AI components?

- Ethics and explainability: How can I contribute to building AI solutions that are transparent, fair and mitigate bias?

Software Tester

The software tester has responsibility for the definition of test cases aligned to the overall quality objectives. They will work to perform tests of various types to provide feedback and quality metrics to the software development team. They should aim to achieve measurable quality objectives such as:

- components of the application/platform—software created, integrated components, databases, user interfaces

- attributes of the application/platform—performance, usability, fitness for purpose

The role of the software tester will evolve into one focused on orchestrating and interpreting generative AI-enabled testing. There will be no reason to manually craft numerous test cases, instead test strategies will be implemented by generating automated tests into a framework. We are already seeing AI-powered tools that can generate extensive test suites. The benefits will be in the ability to cover many more scenarios and help the tester consider the more complex and unpredictable scenarios. Testers will become the curators of generated tests, interpreting the output and using judgment to evaluate the level of quality and coverage.

There will be a huge focus on data quality, and privacy will be crucial. Machine learning capabilities rely on the training data fed into models. Testers will have to work with data engineers to ensure the data used reflects real-world scenarios and edge cases, enabling robust model testing to protect the lifespan of the software.

We will certainly see new requirements emerge in the area of explainable AI (xAI) and I can see that the role of tester will be just as critical to this as the data scientist. New testing paradigms will emerge, specifically designed for AI-enabled systems. Testers will play a pivotal role in executing these methodologies for testing the AI software components and communicating and explaining metrics back to the business to protect against bias and model drift.

Key Decisions for Software Testers to Make

- Upskilling: What specific AI concepts and testing techniques do I need to prioritize for learning?

- xAI metrics: What metrics can I use to measure and track the appropriateness and transparency of the models we develop or use?

- Data expertise: How can I gain the skills to assess training data quality and its impact on AI testing?

- AI component testing: What are the emerging best practices for testing the robustness, explainability and fairness of AI models within a software system?

- Communication: How can I clearly explain the nuances of AI-generated test results and risks to both technical and nontechnical stakeholders?

- Tool Evaluation: How do I assess and select AI testing tools that complement our existing workflows?

TABLE 10 – Summary impacts on the software development team

Critical Component	Impact of AI
Requirements creation	The software architect will have to work with the machine learning and data scientists to identify and select the right AI capabilities to use, while also educating the business stakeholders how to take advantage of these tools. New channels that emerge with use cases that are unfamiliar (conversational UI, virtual assistants, chatBots) will alter the solution stack and force the team to refine all aspects of the architecture to accommodate. Attributes that are well understood for cloud-based software components such as resilience, scalability, security and adaptability will need to be proven for AI tools, and provide the entire development team with a learning curve and introduce some risk into their decision-making.
Solution patterns	The software development team will have proactively reach out to help product management teams refine requirements that are relevent and appropriate for AI solutions. The entire team will definitely benefit from the support that new AI tools will bring, such as carrying out stronger design validation or smoke tests for a logical architecture. We will see more metrics defined around business value estimation and realization due to the potential cost of adding in AI to the application or platform. Software teams will have to embrace the new uncertainty of workflows and business rules that are able to learn at runtime, e.g., identify and remove exceptions from the task flow, intercepting additional manual tasks as the capability allows.

continued ▶

Critical Component	Impact of AI
Software architecture	The software teams will need to work together to think deeply about their existing applications and look for opportunities to integrate with potentially multiple AI tools as a service. The team will have to understand and create the links for new services that will evolve as part of the solution. ML and NLP will drive the evolution initially to enable applications to learn from the user and improve support for the business process. A critical success factor will be in establishing boundaries for the safe use of AI tools. This is not a totally new discipline. Technology teams are used to measuring risk and assessing data security aspects of their design. Managing the ethics around the use of these tools is quite new and will remain a challenge.
Security	It is vital that security and privacy teams provide insight into the guardrails that will help control and consume data where AI tools are used. This team should receive security as a service to facilitate "permission-based everything" for all key dependencies to the software process, e.g., correct access to environments, regular automated user attestation for applications and data privacy controls.
Quality	The team should look for opportunities for AI optimization which will augment and improve the application on the fly as it learns from certain control conditions and parameters. They will be able to prompt the QA teams and business analysts to increase test coverage and go much further into aspects of the application quality such as performance and data security. It is likely that AI-powered QA automation tools will be able to consume APIs and application interfaces at all levels, and proceed to write, execute and report on test scenarios and continuously adapt and improve the coverage and level of testing.
Deployment and DevOps	The team will be served with enhancements and benefit from much stronger insights from real time behavior of the application. This will be driven by the ability to use NLP to query in plain terms without having to build rigid analytics or reports. They will be able to collaborate closely with the DevOps architect to model out various scenarios of deployment to aid in release planning and focus on overall cost management.
Hosting and runtime	They will start to measure software defect impacts and carry out defect impact extrapolation—a term not widely used but introduced here. This is largely manual and subjective today. It will become much more powerful, with AI capabilities seeking to measure downtime, intervention time, workaround time and inform self-healing prioritization. This will appear in both public cloud IaaS platforms (e.g., AWS CloudWatch) and bespoke software.

continued ▶

Critical Component	Impact of AI
Adoption and use	As the AI tools become widespread, pressure will appear from two directions: competitors and startups will launch features extremely rapidly, and end users will be expected to adopt new features faster.
	The roles involved in software design will have to deal with more rapid feedback loops and bigger and faster shifts in the competitive landscape. A new methodology will be needed to support the selection, trialing, proving and adoption of AI tools with end user involvement.
Ongoing maintenance	The team will be provided AI solutions to measure risk within the application itself. These will cover some important risks such as security, including risk of data being leaked, risk of intrusion, risk of downtime from releases/changes/defects or infrastructure failure and risk of low ROI through measuring active use of features and specific scenarios.

4.3 The DevOps and MLOps Teams

DevOps has become a crucial enabler of the growth and success of almost all modern software-centric businesses. If we think of the speed and scale in growth across so many segments of the industry, it has propelled forward almost every important aspect.

- time to market

- quality of software

- meeting security and privacy constraints

- financial economics of offering SaaS

Without an intelligent and complete framework of rules, guidance and automation to help us deliver, society would not see the scope and scale of software success stories that we do today. This book will not attempt to chronicle this field of study here but will comment at the high level and identify the main components you will need to consider when bringing machine learning and AI considerations to the table.

DevOps Architect

The DevOps architect role became mainstream around 2014. It is now critical and sought after with the main responsibility being the design and implementation of scalable secure services that facilitate key aspects of software development, testing and deployment. Typically, the architect will have considerable, hands-on experience of building software and familiarity with the tools and processes facing their DevOps engineers. It is hard to simply gloss over what a DevOps architect looks after because they underpin very important aspects at each stage of the life cycle. The mission critical aspects of the role are captured in figure 23.

DevOps Architect – Best Practices in DevOps

Stage	Core role	How it is done
Strategy & Planning	Develop and implement the overall DevOps strategy and roadmap.	Publish a plan for improving DevOps practices with agreed goals and defined objectives in a time frame.
Tool choice & Implementation	Select and implement appropriate tools and technologies to support the strategy.	Oversee the setup of CI/CD pipelines, implementing code and component automation frameworks, for deployable delivery, management and monitoring.
Leadership & Collaboration	Facilitate good communication across teams with transparency and coordination throughout the software development lifecycle.	Regular team sessions, embrace failure and celebrate wins together, check in with senior leadership to ensure they have the big picture.
Cloud & Infrastructure Management	Responsible for designing and managing the cloud and infrastructure services that support the DevOps practices.	Provision and manage cloud resources, services and infrastructure through repeatable and automated pipelines.
Continuous Improvement	DevOps Architects drive the culture of continuous improvement, increasing automation, addressing failures, removing blockers and using the best tools for the job.	Improve from metrics and visibility into performance of the system from many aspects: response times, failures, security breaches, manual intervention, downtime from defects.
Risk & Security	Ensure the delivery life cycle adheres to security and compliance requirements.	Make constant security checks, harden systems and automate to protect data, applications, and infrastructure from potential threats and vulnerabilities.

FIGURE 23. *DevOps best practices.*

Delivery of AI capabilities incorporating machine learning models and new APIs requires additional skill sets in the software development team. There are additional demands now when creating, managing, deploying and maintaining the machine learning and AI components.

TABLE 11 – Team and Roles to Consider for MLOps

Role and Seniority	Primary Responsibility and Focus	Impact of AI
DevOps Architect Mid-level to Senior	Manage the availability of scalable, secure services that underpin key aspects of the delivery lifecycle	Integrating AI into DevOps will rely on strong collaboration between data scientists. DevOps architects bridge communication gaps between these two disciplines. Will need to manage the complexity and challenge of debugging issues or mitigating potential biases in AI components.
	Evolve and improve CI/CD pipelines to streamline the way software is written, tested and deployed	
DevOps Engineer Mid-level to senior	Implement scalable secure services that facilitate software creation and testing	DevOps engineers should adapt quickly as their tool sets have been constantly evolving and improving the last number of years. They will need to collaborate with both data scientists and machine learning specialists. In larger teams they may have the luxury of working alongside an MLOps resource.
	Use DevOps tools to create and maintain CI/CD pipelines.	
MLOps Engineer Junior to mid-level	Implement scalable and automated services that facilitate AI components and machine learning models	Strong understanding of machine learning concepts and algorithms. They work with machine learning engineers to develop and manage the pipelines for training, testing, and deploying ML models across test, training and production environments.
	Use MLOps tools to create and maintain CI/CD pipelines for the ML and AI components of the solution	

DevOps Engineer

The DevOps engineer has responsibility for implementing and maintaining all tools, services and infrastructure that support the software creation and deployment process. Though the role can vary depending on the makeup of the team and the complexity of the technology stack in use, it invariably involves a combination of release engineering, infrastructure provisioning and management, system administration and security monitoring and management. They should aim to support and guide the software development team to achieve a high level of automation, repeatability and quality throughout the software creation process.

Machine Learning Operations (MLOps) Engineer

The MLOps engineer role is to design, build, run and manage machine learning and AI-based systems. They are responsible for the infrastructure that underpins the ML models and algorithms that are created as part of the machine learning pipeline discussed in chapter 3. In large part, one can safely assume that an organization that will build machine learning models at any scale will already have a DevOps team in place. Any startup that is born as an AI-native should strongly consider having this in place to provide a good foundation for MLOps team members to be a part of.

The Impact on
How We Create Software

*"In the age of AI, software development shifts
from traditional coding to training and guiding
intelligent systems, unlocking new possibilities
and pushing the boundaries of innovation."*

—ERIC SCHMIDT

In this final chapter we look across the software development lifecycle and examine the impacts of AI on how we go about creating business software.

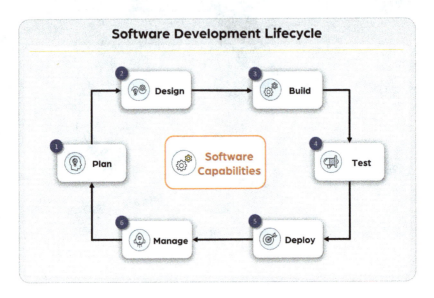

FIGURE 24. *Software life cycle.*

In figure 24 we have a high-level outline view of the software delivery life cycle deliberately abstracted from the methodology. There are two main software development methods, Agile and Waterfall. Most teams nowadays combine the best of both to suit their needs, the type of software they are creating, the complexity of the architecture and also the release cadence they wish to achieve. Most practitioners will already know that the Waterfall model is a linear, sequential approach to software development, where each phase is intended to be completed before the next one begins. In Waterfall, requirements are gathered and documented in detail, and the scope of work is well-defined. Good practice would mean that we would typically have completion criteria defined so that we can exit the planning stage and move into design. Agile is an incremental approach to software development that emphasizes flexibility and adaptability. The delivery of tested software is divided into sprints, which are time-based bursts of activity, typically two to four weeks in length. During each sprint, a small piece of functionality is designed, developed, tested and deployed. The requirements are not usually planned and defined in full detail upfront and can emerge and evolve as part of the sprint.

To help us examine the immediate impacts of AI on the software development process, we use a case study as a frame of reference and discuss some challenges a software team should consider.

CASE STUDY – A successful SaaS provider plans to launch new AI features in its next release.

Company context

BrightIdea is a company operating globally with offices in the US, Brazil, Ireland, London, Bulgaria, Mumbai, Perth and Singapore.

They have a popular SaaS-based application used mainly by finance professionals to automate the management of general ledgers, allowing users and systems to upload or send via API, managing the approval workflow and direct integration with the finance system.

This existing application has a current modern architecture based on cloud and microservices and a high level roadmap looking out twenty-four months.

The AI challenge

Recently, the team hired a data scientist and a machine learning specialist who identified potential AI use cases. One was the integration of a support chatbot with real-time customer data to handle detailed queries about the service, the technical status and troubleshooting any issues. The others were additional, processing flexibility into the maintenance of GL codes and highlighting and detecting trends from the GL data. During a routine planning session, the CPO announces that three of these AI features must be included in the upcoming release to showcase progress to stakeholders. The team now has five months to do so.

TABLE 12 – summary of the immediate considerations for including AI features.

Stage	Key Questions
Plan	Should existing stories be removed to accommodate the new AI features?
	Has it been decided to publicly launch the AI features or will this be a beta launch?
	Will the machine learning model be integrated and trained in time?
	Where will we acquire the data or will we leverage an open-source LLM to assist in powering the generation of the responses?

continued ▶

Stage	Key Questions
Design	First step is to rapidly run a spike to investigate whether to leverage open-source models and algorithms or fine tune a model in-house.
	We will need new API definitions to allow parallel development.
	The machine learning team may decide to stick to intents (e.g., "track order", "check balance") and data entities to use (e.g., order number, account ID) to answer the operational queries.
	How will we handle unexpected responses from the model?
	An important security by design principle is to ensure no risk of data breach.
	We will need to invest in some MLOps skill sets to align with the tools used for DevOps in the existing platform management.
	Performance and stress tests will need to be planned to ensure scalability.
Build	Can the machine learning models achieve the required accuracy and precision within the deadline?
	Early API definition will ensure the application development team can progress in collaboration with the machine learning team.
	The data architect will be assigned to design the pipeline to structure and transform the feed for real-time consumption.
	Data will be necessary for training and validation. Do we build synthetic data, use existing data or leverage free/open-source data from public sources?
Test	Ensure that customer data is anonymized for training and testing the new model.
	Validate that it is not possible to regenerate or reverse engineer personal identifiable information from the models.
	Can we use manual QA while the test team develops the automated test framework hooks?
	How will we define and evaluate user interactions with the model?
Deploy	Can we integrate the machine learning components into the DevOps pipeline, or will manual deployment be necessary for this release?
	The data scientist has planned leave during the production deployment—this is a risk.
Manage	How will the machine learning team monitor the health of the ML components without access to the production environment?
	Is a security and privacy assessment required for the new customer data generated by the chatbot and model?
	How will we intervene or override inaccurate responses?

In figure 25, we propose a view to help bring these key elements together.

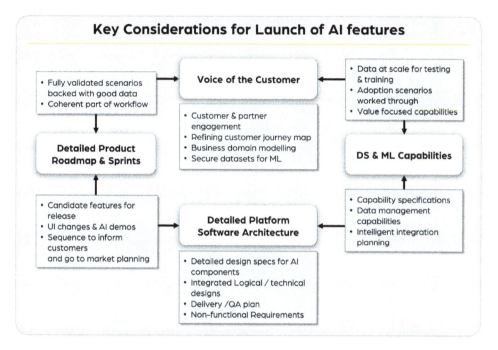

Key Considerations for Launch of AI features

- Fully validated scenarios backed with good data
- Coherent part of workflow

Voice of the Customer

- Data at scale for testing & training
- Adoption scenarios worked through
- Value focused capabilities

- Customer & partner engagement
- Refining customer journey map
- Business domain modelling
- Secure datasets for ML

Detailed Product Roadmap & Sprints

DS & ML Capabilities

- Candidate features for release
- UI changes & AI demos
- Sequence to inform customers and go to market planning

Detailed Platform Software Architecture

- Capability specifications
- Data management capabilities
- Intelligent integration planning

- Detailed design specs for AI components
- Integrated Logical / technical designs
- Delivery /QA plan
- Non-functional Requirements

FIGURE 25. *Key Considerations for Launch of AI features*

Impact on Planning

We should consider planning to encompass the broad definition of both the scoping activities as inputs into release cycles/sprints and the steering and governance of the product roadmap and alignment with the business strategy. From a product management perspective, there will be pressure to include AI features into the architecture because of potential benefits internally or for customer experience, along with pressure from shareholders and senior leadership to maintain alignment with competitors and the wider industry. Already we are seeing AI-enabled tools emerging that can help manage customer insights and this feedback loop including Dovetail, a user research platform, Zelta AI, which takes insights from sales calls, and unit Q, which asks for user feedback.

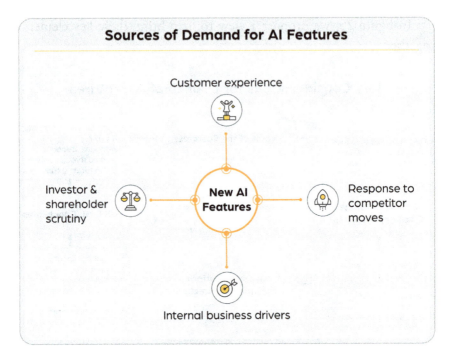

FIGURE 26. *Sources of demand.*

It's going to be important for product managers to balance this pressure to include AI features by assessing the real business value on offer, and ensuring the technical teams can deliver the solution! It's clear from our case study that there are fundamental decisions to be tackled when starting out with new AI initiatives. In the planning stage, especially when getting started, there will be enabling and limiting factors to understand in the context of your team. It starts with a positive investment appetite and moves quickly into being specific about what the scope will be and what business benefit will be targeted. Obviously, having the right skills will be fundamental, but then incorporating these skills into the organization's life cycle will be a challenge. The availability of the right data is an absolute must, along with having the budget to cover the hardware and compute resources to develop, train and test models. Appropriate data privacy controls and security constraints will apply to the business use cases and data used.

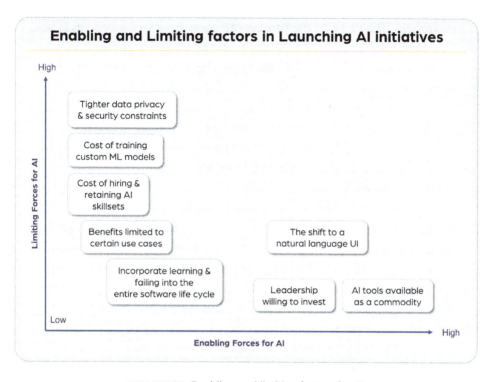

FIGURE 27. *Enabling and limiting factors for AI.*

Generative AI is already being used by most software teams worldwide. In a survey in 2023, GitHub found that 92 percent of engineering teams are already using AI tools at work. As AI tools become more of a commodity, some of the choices and decisions will be made harder than ever. There will be an opportunity to look for points of difference in safety guardrails and alignment with trust and security standards. The natural language UI will fall into the trap of being used everywhere, even where it offers no significant value. How many websites now offer some form of AI enabled chat bot that pops a little message asking how it can help.

We can foresee that AI tools will become the "voice of the process" in software development. This concept from Six Sigma gives us a way of measuring how successfully we achieve outcomes and surface up metrics to drive decision making and improvements. I recommend readers check this out—it is often overshadowed by the "voice of the customer." The voice of the process can show how well a process is being performed in real time. It can help understand variability, or why things are going wrong. By listening to the voice of the process, decision-makers can identify variations and deviations from the expected outcome. It brings data-driven decision-making to the fore, avoiding assumptions or perceptions. Imagine a busy product manager with a team of twenty on their wider software team. The promise of being able to have a natural language-based conversation with rich data to understand how their team is doing would be extremely powerful. They could look to identify expensive bottlenecks in how work is being allocated, find patterns in how critical defects originate. Going further, the voice of process supported by an ML tool could calculate and display important metrics like work-in-progress limits that are often simply not used because they are hard to measure. All of this can be enabled by the ingestion of lots of structured and unstructured data into the generative AI tools that are already being used every day for increased productivity. Plug and play integrations with sources such as AWS CodePipeline, Azure DevOps, GitHub, CircleCI and Octopus Deploy will mean that deep data on delivery velocity, software development, code management activity, testing activity, defects, outages, issues and deployments from previous releases will all be available.

Questions that product managers and scrum masters can then ask:

- Is the release timeline viable based on historic trends and current resources?

- Who are the top performers on the team?

- Which team members need more support?

- Present insights into what components of the system are prone to the most errors

It is likely that as AI services become commoditized, the choice and number of available components and solution options will complicate the planning process. Radical shifts based on new capabilities or competitor behavior have to be expected and embraced as facts of life. That important product roadmap item that was well-planned eight or ten months ago may become obsolete in the space of a week. The planning activity will have to include a degree of flexibility. I foresee an opportunity to create a distinct AI strategy team that could act as the "headlights in the night". This small team could be asked to regularly assess the market for developments and check the impact on the company's business model and technical vision. I am already using this principle in a startup I am involved in, and it is proving to be a very useful way to manage the sheer volume of developments that are being announced. This blizzard of marketing in the wave of change is not unique to AI, but the timelines for change and the potential stakes will be higher this time around.

We can see a trend where software delivery teams will receive a great deal more useful feedback and insights from their application and platform stacks. Today this is geared towards technical infrastructure metrics using application performance management (APM) tools such as Amazon CloudWatch, New Relic, Splunk, Grafana and others. This trend will quickly evolve to offer business-level insights and natural language query and interrogation capabilities. It will drive a new level of understanding into how applications and platforms are meeting business and operational objectives such as customer satisfaction in business outcomes, error rates in the business process, percent of task automation and time taken to complete tasks. The trend will blur the lines in roles and responsibilities across delivery which we examine in the next chapter. Eventually, generative AI will be used extensively to co-author and validate almost every structured deliverable involved in the planning stage. It will offer users insight and feedback during their working day to become more productive. We can see intelligent plan management intervening to help task owners stay focused with nudges and reminders to complete tasks on the critical path.

To conclude the planning section, in figure 28, I present an outline framework as a starting point to help when planning investments into AI. This table will help as a pointer in posing questions and identifying important considerations.

STAGES	IDENTIFY	EXPERIMENT	LAUNCH	LEARN	SCALE
Focus Activities	• Define the AI strategy • Identify high-impact use cases for AI • Assign early resources • Form Investment thesis	• Run POCs • Model prototyping • Performance testing • Cost assessments • Planning for launch	• Deployment (pilot or full-scale) • User training • Integration with existing systems	• Performance monitoring • Feedback collection (users & KPIs) • Model refinement as needed	• Expand usage across the organization • Automate data collection & model updates
Input	• Outline business needs & opportunities • Available data sources • Funding • Tools	• Small-scale datasets • AI tools / frameworks • Technical & business KPIs • Data privacy assessment	• Production-ready AI models • Cost projections • Data privacy management	• Real-world usage & feedback • Sharp performance metrics • Dialogue with users	• Proven AI use cases • Robust MLOps processes • Promote buy-in across teams
Teams Involved	**Lead:** Business SME, Data Science & ML Leads **Support:** Data science & ML teams	**Lead:** Data Science & ML Teams **Support:** Business Unit SME, Software Teams	**Lead:** ML & DevOps **Support:** Data Science & ML Teams, Business Unit SME & End Users	**Lead:** Data Science & ML Teams **Support:** Business Units, ML and DevOps	**Lead:** Data science & ML teams, ML & DevOps **Support:** Business units, software Teams
Outcomes	• Prioritized list of potential projects • ML architecture • Spin up infrastructure	• Options on viable AI models • Cost-benefit analysis	• Viable AI models • Insights on performance • Cost-benefit analysis	• Model accuracy • Actions for further optimization • Rolling ROI assessment	• Wider business impact from AI • Metric driven decisions • Benefits realization

AI Investment Journey

FIGURE 28. *Investment framework.*

Impact on Design

One of the biggest impacts that AI is having on software design is in the revisions to existing design patterns and principles. They include:

- More dynamic data. AI introduces new design patterns that can handle dynamic and unstructured data more effectively. This will enable us to design systems that will adapt to changing data patterns over time and open up new possibilities in how software reacts to those changes.

- Integration of machine learning models. Design patterns will start to accommodate the integration of machine learning models seamlessly into software systems. We can already see approaches being taken which consider the machine learning models as intelligent APIs.

- Enhanced user experience. The power and efficiency of natural language processing is changing the way we use technology forever. By lowering the threshold of consumption, the ability of our species to be able to construct and execute new types of software will expand and increase at rates we cannot yet imagine.

- Real-time decisions. AI capabilities are starting to allow us to consider the implementation of capabilities within software systems that will support efficient processing of streaming data and rapid response to changing conditions.

- Explainability and transparency. Regulatory and governance forces will drive the industry to prioritize explainability and transparency, allowing users to understand how algorithms make decisions and providing mechanisms for auditing and debugging AI systems.

- Scalability and resource efficiency. Design patterns will be needed to address the resource efficiency of AI-driven systems, including distributed computing architectures, parallel processing and optimization techniques to handle large-scale data processing and analysis.

- Adversarial robustness. Security by design patterns will have to consider the potential weaknesses of AI models to attack. New techniques will be needed for improving robustness and resilience against malicious exploitation. We must assume the worst is going to happen and work back from there unfortunately.

- Continuous learning and adaptation. We have seen that AI systems are beginning to support continuous learning, offering an opportunity for the software to improve its performance over time through feedback loops. There will be demand for automated ways of refreshing ML models and support updates/retraining to help with evolving user preferences and environmental conditions.

- Ethical and legal considerations. Hopefully, we will see consumer and government intervention to put trust and privacy protection, bias mitigation, fairness, accountability and compliance to the forefront of requirements for AI-powered software.

Agents and Agentic Systems

This is a very interesting emerging design pattern. Agents are intelligent software components designed to be capable of reasoning about their observations and acting upon them to achieve desired outcomes. These agents can use a variety of techniques, including machine learning, natural language processing and symbolic reasoning. One example of an agent will be in the emergence of intelligent containers and APIs that will observe and learn from software behavior in production. The agents will be granted permission and the ability to inspect interfaces between components in real time. The purpose of this is to monitor the exchange of data packets, understand why errors happen within the software and trace how APIs and functions are invoked. The agent could be designed to look for ways to optimize the composition and arrangement of components in real time. This could be extended to allow for self-healing in the case of outages and for robustness to hacking.

Retaining Compatibility will be a Challenge

Machine learning and data science pipelines differ somewhat from software code development and CI/CD pipelines. They are more data intensive, requiring training and test phases. The resulting model may not even get deployed if accuracy targets cannot be achieved. We are going to see new types of machine learning models appear that do not exist today. These new capabilities could potentially mean that existing trained models such as LLMs are redundant. Imagine the disruption in terms of loss of return on investment? This scenario would inevitably force a major decision on compatibility. Do we break with the existing model type or move to the new model and lose the "heritage?"

In the future, architects will be able to use natural language to get insight into the "voice of the process" in terms of key progress and outcome metrics, e.g., exception rates, manual intervention time and automation percent of total workflows. Other metrics, even system and error logs from available technical and business sources, will be ingested and used to extrapolate and create different scenarios to compare design proposals. Black box AI tools will come up with recommended enhancements or fresh designs when providing new business requirements together and a picture of a baseline architecture. Explainable artificial intelligence (xAI) will offer a white box equivalent to the black box above and will be like a wise mentor carefully explaining in detail why it chose an alternative solution or suggested an enhancement. There will be some complex questions to answer in the stage of the software cycle over the ethical use of data when designing AI software solutions. It is also highly likely that data privacy legislation will erode the ability to continue to use the same data over extended periods to power machine learning models. How will we bake in the right to be forgotten as we develop more complex machine learning models? This concept, also known as the right to erasure, allows individuals to request the removal of their personal data from search engines and other online platforms. Applying this right to our AI models trained on large datasets will pose challenges. We may not be able to identify and remove specific data points, because in an AI model it is difficult to isolate and remove individual contributions.

Customers and end users will want to know how their data is being used in AI. Transparency will be crucial for building and maintaining trust. Caution, more challenges ahead! Explaining where data is used and how can be difficult. We have already explored where the physical makeup of models can be intricate, making it difficult to explain their actual internal workings in a clear and comprehensible manner. In revealing specific data points, we could even risk compromising the privacy of individuals used to train the model. Removing any data could very well negatively impact the accuracy and effectiveness of the solution, providing a force of resistance to do so. The oversight is only going to get tougher and tighter. Already we have the General Data Protection Regulation (GDPR), the Data Governance Act (DORA) and the AI Act in the EU which lay out strict guidelines for data protection and responsible AI development. These frameworks require organizations to:

- implement data governance practices to oversee data collection, storage, and usage

- conduct privacy impact assessments to evaluate potential risks associated with AI models and show how these risks will be mitigated

- actively demonstrate fairness and how there is no discrimination or bias present in the development and use of AI systems

- monitor AI models and networks for data leakage and misuse

The EU AI Act is a new regulation passed by the European Union aimed at governing the development and use of AI in the software ecosystem. It takes a risk-based approach, classifying AI systems into different risk categories.

- **Unacceptable Risk**
  AI systems which are deemed a threat to safety, livelihoods, or rights are completely banned, which is a great move.

- **High-Risk**
  AI embedded in software for critical sectors like healthcare, transportation or law enforcement will face strict requirements for transparency, data quality, and human oversight.

- **Limited Risk**
  Systems like chatbots have transparency obligations to inform the end user that they are interacting with AI software.

- **Minimal Risk**
  Most of the current AI applications will land here initially. As a result, they will face minimal legal requirements. We predict this will change, the typical approach for lawmakers is to encroach slowly and carefully.

The AI act is a very welcome development, and much like GDPR it is expected to become a global benchmark for AI regulation, hopefully influencing similar legislation worldwide.

A common theme in technology is that where there is a recognized need there will be a surge in offerings to help businesses fulfill their requirements. Due to the security and privacy imperatives, feature sets will emerge to help preserve data privacy in AI. We will need to see stronger data anonymization techniques to balance the protection of sensitive data while preserving its value in training purposes.

One possibility is to inject statistical noise into data, preventing the extraction of individual information. Another idea might be to monetize data for training so that consumers are offered some sort of financial reward in return for their data. Could this look like recent crypto developments in decentralized finance where you receive a financial interest rate for staking crypto currency for a period of time? When machine learning and data science experts complete their privacy impact assessments, regulatory bodies will have to trust them. Given the complexity of translating the technical aspects, it may be very difficult for these experts to prove that they are acting in the best interests of their profession.

Impact on Build

The impact of AI on the software build stage will be comprehensive. We briefly touched on the impact at the top of the chapter, and it is going to disrupt many of the processes involved in building software solutions. Due to the structured nature of the domain, code generation, code review and documentation tasks can be objectively measured, considering key aspects such as code correctness, completeness, adherence to standards and documentation clarity. All these tasks are very well suited to being achieved at scale with the latest generative AI models. This area of software has attracted a huge amount of attention in the media, with almost nonstop news feeds announcing new AI-powered coding tools. In terms of the real impact on the software build stage, there have been some notable and powerful advances in tooling.

OpenAI Codex is a powerful model trained on a massive dataset of code and natural language. It can use this to produce code snippets depending on developer inputs supplied in natural language. Codex can be used in various contexts such as in developer environment plugins, text editors or custom applications. It is based on GTP-3 and is available to use via API. There are some interesting tools being built on top of Codex, namely Pygma, which uses Codex to turn Figma designs into different front-end frameworks, and Replit which describes what a segment of code is doing in simple language. Codex is also powering the next tool in the list which has exploded into widespread use.

GitHub Copilot, launched in June 2021, is now the world's most widely adopted AI programming tool. The tool is an evolution of the "Bing Code Search" plugin for Visual Studio 2013 but is now based on OpenAI Codex along with additional fine tuning and training. GitHub CoPilot is an AI pair programmer that offers autocomplete suggestions as a developer works within their development environment. Suggestions come inline from Copilot as code is written, or the developer can write a natural language prompt describing what they want the software code to do. In November 2023, Copilot was updated to use OpenAI's Codex model, which itself has been trained on billions of lines of open-source code. GitHub Copilot is not perfect (nothing is in the world of AI!) and can contain coding patterns that may not be fully secure. There may be inherent bugs in the logic, or it might include references to outdated APIs. A key positive feature of Copilot is that it learns from the code included in the repository, so it can use this to provide more accurate suggestions. This can be helpful for developers who work on large, complicated projects where context is important.

CodeT5 is a free, open-source tool created by data scientists at Salesforce. Their goal was to address some of the shortcomings in other AI coding tools. They wanted the tool to focus more on the actual programming languages and not rely as heavily on natural language processing in their training data. CodeT5 can generate new code, perform code summarization, code refinement and carry out translation from one language to another. It has encoder and decoder models that it uses to translate natural language into code and translate code back into natural language. This feature is highly useful, not least for a new developer joining a team who is being asked to maintain code written by someone else.

Codiga helps teams place a strong emphasis on quality and security. This AI-powered code assistant is more focused on code review than code generation. It can review and auto-fix any issues it finds, and it can be taught new code review rules that the developer would like to add. It also inspects software for common security threats and can automatically fix vulnerabilities. These types of tools will quickly become indispensable for developers, and possibly mandatory as part of enterprise software teams. We can foresee tools such as this one being enabled to protect the integrity of the process so that no personally identifiable data is used in the development or testing of code.

All these tools underline the trend towards assisted coding. Teams are looking for help with quality and consistency along with some increase in quantity and velocity of code output. Natural language processing techniques can:

- generate code snippets from high level descriptions

- produce longer code modules from detailed requirements and well-constructed prompts

- extract meaningful information from code comments and function signatures inline in the code itself

- use the code structure to generate documentation that is clear, accurate and up-to-date

- debug intelligently (looking at error messages, stack traces and code context to suggest potential root causes and solutions)

The main impacts and benefits that will accrue in the short term will mean software developers can crystallize their ideas more quickly by auto-generating the scaffolding code to form outline solution components. They can move faster at ticking off the mundane or repetitive tasks. They can also leverage the tools for basic bug fixing, consistency analysis and documentation tasks. This may not immediately reduce the time to market for solutions. It certainly will not remove the need for human developers. We are seeing some evidence that using these tools increases job satisfaction and gives developers back time to think about their outcomes and form ideas on solving the business problem at hand. These benefits might be hard to quantify in dollar terms, but they are very important to the community of people that write software for a living.

Impact on Testing

Rightly or wrongly, in many organizations, the roles of test analyst or QA engineer have been considered less prestigious than the role of software engineer. Having worked as a tester for a short time in my career, it taught me an invaluable discipline to double check the basic quality of your output and to reflect on what the output will mean to the person you are creating it for. This was a great habit to adopt and is transferable to almost any human endeavor.

There is an opportunity now with AI tools and approaches to truly highlight the added value of the testing discipline. We propose that QA teams seize this opportunity with both hands, build their profile, emphasize the value they bring and highlight how they protect the business operation. I believe there could be a more positive impact in this stage than in many of the other stages, augmenting the impact of human workers more than replacing them. The impact of AI in software testing will be a classic case of "more please!" Using generative AI to create volumes of executable automated tests? This will be a significant and powerful shift beyond what teams of human testers can achieve. Embedding an AI powered tool alongside current toolsets will also help avoid disruption and reduce barriers to acceptance.

Here are some frameworks to consider.

Test Automation Frameworks

- Applitools: the old reliable open-source framework for automating tests
- Appium: open-source framework for cross-platform mobile app testing on iOS and Android devices

- Cypress: JavaScript-based framework designed for fast, reliable and developer-friendly end-to-end web testing

- Robot Framework: keyword-driven Python-based framework for test automation, adaptable to various testing needs

A constant challenge in achieving good test coverage is creating and managing data that can be used to execute meaningful tests. This is one area where the tools and the people skills can be applied to generating realistic test data to find issues before release.

AI is poised to revolutionize data generation to help QA teams with the following approaches.

Synthetic Data Generation

Depending on your view, this is possibly the biggest opportunity and threat for AI in software. If we consider generative adversarial networks (GANs), which can learn the underlying patterns and distributions of real-world data, it is very possible they could be used to generate new synthetic datasets that are statistically similar to production data, while preserving privacy. This would empower human testers to be massively productive, and manage a mathematical "to the power of" array of test cases. Imagine two testers able to generate 500 valid tests using AI each day for a month (assuming 20 working days on average). This would be 20,000 executable, automated tests for a software application. This would offer amazing test coverage of any software application.

On the flip side, data scientists will tell us that using synthetic data is dangerous when training models and can cause bias, lack of generalization and hallucination. There have been many commentators suggesting that Gemini's recent fax pax in advising people to use glue to stick cheese to pizza was caused by training the model with synthetic data. There are some techniques that can help here—there are ML algorithms that can manipulate existing test datasets to expand their scope and variety. Techniques like image rotation, noise injection or text transformations have helped create the latest most popular large language models.

ML models can also be used to analyze large production datasets and to identify the most impactful and representative subsets for testing.

Some emerging trends in testing are worth summarizing here:

- Code Scanning. Machine learning models will scan/ingest source code and test case repositories, historical code changes, and documentation and combine knowledge of best practices to spot and predict defects. The ability to scan code will help continuously to expand test coverage and generate valid edge cases that would take QA analysts many working hours to cover.

- Real-time Dynamic Analysis. Already, there are tools like DeepCode and Fortify which can analyze program behavior at runtime, detecting vulnerabilities and security exploits.

- Test Case Generation. Tools such as DeepTest and SmartTest automatically generate comprehensive ranges of tests to increase test coverage. These tools can also be used to align testing suites to match production use and load scenarios.

- Predictive Testing. Models will be used to predict areas in the code base and architecture that are more prone to bugs, allowing developers to prioritize their unit testing efforts and improve code quality. There is also an opportunity to remove unnecessary tests and reduce maintenance costs by auto-updating outdated test scripts.

The latest and most popular tools that should be considered for software testing in the new era are outlined below:

Performance and Load Testing

- JMeter—open-source Java-based tool for load testing and analyzing application performance

- k6—modern developer-centric load testing tool using JavaScript and streamlined scripting

- Gatling—Scala-based tool for load testing focused on high performance and developer-friendly code

- LoadRunner—Micro Focus tool offering a comprehensive suite for enterprise-level performance testing (a classic tool for this problem statement, but there will be many open-source options)

Test Management and Collaboration

- Jira (with Confluence and testing plugins)—issue-tracking tool extensible for test management with various plugins and integrations

- TestRail—centralized web-based test case management platform for tracking test plans, execution and reports

- Xray—Jira-native test management app for comprehensive test planning and reporting

Impact on Deploy

At this stage of the software creation cycle, if we are following best practice, we should have well-tested and validated software components ready to push to a production environment. This transition to production should be a well-rehearsed and mostly automated pipeline. As AI components have been largely born into a cloud-native world, it is not unusual to expect that they will be ready to incorporate into existing deployment tools and methods. Continuous integration/continuous deployment (CI/CD) is really the fundamental DevOps approach to incremental software code changes which are managed frequently and reliably in an automated way. Our traditional software development CI/CD processes often fall short when dealing with ML models because of their unique characteristics. A discipline which has evolved to bridge the gap between data science, software engineering and DevOps by setting out principles for CI/CD pipelines for machine learning components, MLOps aims to solve some impacting challenges:

- Data dependencies: ML models rely heavily on data sets for training and testing.

- Data scientists and ML engineers have to experiment and tweak various parts of the solution, e.g., hyperparameters, and keep track of the data and the code base to be able to reproduce results.

- Continuous learning and improvement: Machine learning models are not static, and therefore require ongoing monitoring, training and optimization to maintain their effectiveness over time.

The MLOps processes are covering the entire life cycle to protect against these challenges, ensuring that the entire software solution that produces the results in training and testing is what gets deployed into production. It is increasingly more important to monitor the behavior of models in production as part of MLOps, as they can degrade in performance for many reasons including bias and unanticipated inputs in the real world.

Here are some of the latest tools that are in active use by many MLOPs teams:

Open source MLOps tools and pipelines

- Prefect—tool for building and managing end-to-end ML pipelines

- Kubeflow—platform for deploying and managing ML workflows on Kubernetes

- Metaflow—framework for building data science workflows and managing ML deployments

- Flyte—platform for defining, executing and managing data pipelines and workflows

- ZenML—for building modular and collaborative machine learning pipelines

- Pachyderm—data version control system for managing ML data lineage and reproducibility

Experiment Tracking and Model Metadata Management

- MLflow—open-source platform for managing the ML life cycle, including experiment tracking, model registry and deployment

- Comet ML—platform for experiment tracking, comparison, explanation and optimization of ML models

- Weights and biases—ML platform for experiment tracking, data and model versioning, hyperparameter tuning and model management

Model Deployment and Serving

- Amazon SageMaker—managed service for building, training and deploying ML models on AWS

- Google Cloud Vertex AI—unified environment for building, deploying and managing ML models on GCP

- Microsoft Azure machine learning—cloud service for managing the ML life cycle on Azure

- Knative Serving—open-source framework for deploying containerized ML models in production

- Seldon Core: open-source framework for deploying and managing ML models on Kubernetes

Monitoring and Observability

- Neptune.ai—platform for monitoring and managing ML experiments, models and infrastructure

- Paperspace Gradient—platform for experiment tracking, model training and deployment monitoring

- Evidently—open-source library for monitoring and debugging ML models in production

Impact on Manage

Operational teams that support and manage software products, platforms and solutions at scale have undergone many waves of change in the last couple of decades. When the Information Technology Infrastructure Library (ITIL v3) was launched in 2007, it played a key role in bringing a detailed discipline and framework to the way the software profession organized our technology assets. Together with the Control Objectives for Information and Related Technologies (COBIT), these frameworks helped mature how we transitioned, how we managed the processes involved in supporting outages, incidents and downtime. This was important when software was less automated because manual deployments had to be rehearsed, and monolithic releases were often incapable of being rolled back once started. This rigorous control helped to commoditize the effort and skill sets needed to manage the different layers of infrastructure, hardware, platforms, databases and applications that were required to run a modern business

at some level of scale. It allowed many enterprise and corporate businesses to outsource their IT and applications and use them to help with
change management, security, and upgrade and enhancement.

Nowadays, there are fewer reasons to have a detailed and rigorous
framework in place. Business users are more tech savvy, and adopting software tools is mandatory. Either way, employees embrace and
expect the best tools for their work. Cloud-based SaaS products such
as ServiceNow (Salesforce), Zendesk and Prometheus help prescribe
a familiar way of working as standard operating procedure. DevOps
practices have automated and increased the frequency of feature deployment and businesses have embraced this change. So I would con-
tend that unless you work in the public sector (which typically follows
technology trends a little slower than other sectors), your organization
is very likely to already have a mature approach to how they manage
software operations.

AI will bring new considerations to how we manage software and
technology operations. On the positive side, AI tools will give operations teams a much deeper insight into how software components
behave in production systems, and therefore offer better control. AI
will offer the ability to delegate certain decisions to an intelligent platform that will adapt to planned and rehearsed scenarios and learn
and intercept unseen scenarios. Here are some of the exciting features
ahead:

- **Advanced monitoring and anomaly detection**
  Merging complex event processing, business activity
  monitoring, application performance monitoring and
  machine learning models will create massive demand for the
  next generation of software in observability and intelligence
  suites. These tools will be able to subscribe and ingest all sorts
  of events from event clouds and powerful algorithms and
  machine learning to divine insights or monitor transactions
  in real time. Key players to watch are Dynatrace, Datadog,
  Splunk and NewRelic.

- **Continuous feedback on quality and security**
  We will see a huge leap in the use of synthetic, automated testing with the ability to generate and run these tests at scale. Security monitoring organizations will also be able to leverage generative AI tools to formulate robust security screening capabilities and carry out perimeter and penetration testing at much greater scale and depth. Key players to watch are Cisco AppDynamics, Solarwinds and Splunk.

- **Automated cost monitoring and ML management**
  When the cloud began to gain traction, there were fears about costs spiraling out of control. This is still an active risk for many organizations. The level of competitive tension between the major hyperscalers such as Amazon and Microsoft have reduced the impact somewhat, however, it is still taking time to work its way into corporate business case models. There are now categories of tools called "cloud cost management platforms." The same trend will happen with AI. For cost reasons, most businesses will have to initially avoid any large-scale training of machine learning models. They will have to leverage foundation models and open-source equivalents. The good news is that the high demand for AI cost management capabilities will cause several elegant solutions to extend into this space and assist with managing the cost of running models—either in the cloud or in-house. Key players to watch are Cloudhealth, Flexera, Apptio and Nutanix.

AI will also bring forward some considerations, with possible negative consequences. Certain organizations will deliberately lag in AI adoption this very reason: to avoid potential disruption. There are some factors which indicate that an organization is in the manage stage of their software life cycle, and these factors are:

- Industry type—Customer expectations and support needs can vary between industries.

- Company size and resources—Smaller organizations have fewer resources to invest in technology or training.

- Support model—It makes a big difference if operations are managed in-house versus outsourced. Forcing change on an outsourcing partner can be difficult.

Conclusion

At the end of the day, most AI technology is still just software. It is software in a new form that is radically different from the trillions of lines of code that people have spent decades imagining, writing and testing. In this book we have explored the genesis of AI and machine learning from the early days. We have opened the box to understand how the latest large language models and generative AI tools work.

We have looked at the impact of AI on the people who create software. The years 2024 to 2027 will completely alter this landscape. There are two main scenarios. One is a world where it becomes possible for more and more people to be involved in the process of building solutions with technology. This offers new possibilities for individuals and for society. The other is a dystopian world in which well-funded corporations drive the creation of AI enabled software that removes the need for many people to be employed. Emerging nations with large populations would be most impacted.

We discussed the process of how we develop modern software and looked at where AI is going to play a role in shaping the future. There are many tools emerging which will help us create better software much faster. Surely this offers us a massive opportunity to solve seriously difficult problems in healthcare, energy and climate change? In a capitalist world the investment fund will flow where the returns are greatest, and I remain optimistic that these areas will be rich in opportunity and growth.

We also looked at how AI will alter the shape and behavior of the software we create. Starting at the edge, nudging its way into most software platforms and applications through APIs, machine learning will eventually become just a standard piece of software like a database or a front end. It is exciting to think how we will use software through more natural interfaces like everyday language. This will propel us forward in being able to adopt and harness powerful technologies like never before.

We have learned enough in our brief exploration to know that we are still in the very early stages of AI capability. We are still far away from anything close to software enabling general intelligence with the proper reasoning that would resemble the human brain. We have only started to make inroads into the rich sensory world that humans are capable of processing—our sight, hearing, touch, taste and our sense of space and time. It is logical to think that AI is going to have a noticeable impact on how people are rewarded for their technology skills. We can't predict with certainty, though it seems reasonable that those gifted with technical abilities will become much more important in the workplace. Anyone who avoids or resists adopting these new tools could well see a negative impact on their careers.

We all need to participate in shaping the direction that AI evolves in. It will become an important part of the technology ecosystem that we have created to support our advancement as a species. The space is moving so fast it can be hard to keep pace. I believe strongly that a focus on the three fundamental pillars of People, Process and Technology will continue to serve us well in maintaining a balance as we advance. People should be the priority in our future, and not simply as end users or customers but as custodians of skills, value and worth.

I hope that I have offered some small level of insight, posed some questions for the reader to consider, and offered approaches to breaking the problem down into understandable chunks. The next chapter of this story belongs to us all—the coders, the visionaries, the business leaders and the everyday users of this new transformative power. As AI continues to evolve, it will undoubtedly shape how we live and work. I urge you to start the journey and play your role in shaping the future of AI in this new era.

Alternative Conclusion Written by Gemini AI

The following is a playful alternative ending that I asked Gemini, Google's AI assistant, to generate while providing the text of my own conclusion as input into the prompt.

The Clock is Ticking, The Canvas is Blank

Throughout this book, we've unearthed the origins of AI and glimpsed the staggering potential of the tools within our grasp. We've witnessed how AI disrupts the very act of creating software, reshaping our roles and redefining what's possible. The next three years are a count-down—a pivotal moment for individuals and society as a whole. The pace of change is dizzying, yet we are only scratching the surface of AI's true power. Today's machines remain far removed from the nuanced reasoning and rich sensory experiences that make us human. Even so, they are already redrawing the boundaries of our world. A divide is emerging. Those who harness AI as an extension of their skills will gain an unprecedented edge. Time once lost to mundane tasks will be reclaimed for innovation, deeper thinking, and the moments that truly matter. Those who resist will be left behind, potentially facing setbacks in their careers and their ability to navigate an AI-infused world. AI's evolution is a story with countless authors. The tech-savvy will hold greater sway, but this isn't a tale for coders alone. Dreamers, leaders, everyday users—everyone has a voice in this unfolding narrative. The beauty and the danger of AI lie in its reflection of ourselves. Will we use it for greater good or allow it to amplify existing disparities? Will we foster collaboration or competition? The choices we make today will echo for generations.

This book has been a primer, a spark to ignite your curiosity. But the greatest lessons are yet to be written. The future of AI is a vast, uncharted territory. As a reader, you are now an explorer. Discover how AI intersects with your passions, your skills, your sphere of influence. Be bold enough to shape the technology and in turn, shape a better world for us all.

Main Types of Neural Networks

There are many types of artificial neural networks (ANNs) that exist today and we will see an explosion of these in the coming years as the cloud of investment dollars rains down on the industry. Here we run through the main types to help the reader understand the acronyms.

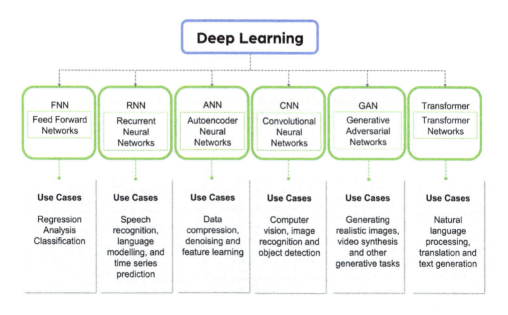

Deep learning models are a subset of ANNs and these are capable of learning complex patterns and representations from data to then provide various types of output functions. Some common types of deep learning models include:

- Feedforward neural networks (FNNs): These are the simplest form of deep neural networks, consisting of multiple layers of neurons where information flows in one direction, from input to output without cycles or loops. They are commonly used for tasks like classification and regression.

- Recurrent neural networks (RNNs): RNNs are designed to handle sequential data where the order of inputs matters. They have loops within their architecture that allow them to retain information over time. RNNs are commonly used for tasks like speech recognition, language modeling and time series prediction.

  - Long short-term memory networks (LSTMs): LSTMs are a type of RNN that addresses the vanishing gradient problem that can occur in traditional RNNs when training on long sequences of data. LSTMs incorporate memory cells and gating mechanisms to selectively remember or forget information over time, making them effective for tasks involving long-range dependencies.

  - Gated recurrent units (GRUs): GRUs are similar to LSTMs and also address the vanishing gradient problem. They have a simpler architecture with fewer parameters, making them computationally more efficient than LSTMs while still being effective for sequential data processing tasks.

- Convolutional neural networks (CNNs): CNNs are specifically designed for processing structured, grid-like data, such as images. They are called convolutional because of the mathematical operation employed at their core. Convolution is an operation that combines two functions to produce a third function. In a CNN, one function is the input image and the other is a filter. The filter slides across the entire input image, performing mathematical processing between the elements in the filter and the elements in the input image. The process is repeated as the filter slides across the entire image, generating an entire feature map. Multiple filters are used, each capturing different features like edges, textures or colors. These are then stacked together to form a higher dimensional representation of the input image. The convolution operations allow the models to learn and process visual information, making them very successful in image-related tasks like computer vision, image recognition and object detection.

- Autoencoders: Autoencoders are unsupervised learning models that aim to learn efficient representations of input data by compressing it into a lower-dimensional latent space and then reconstructing the original input from this representation. They are used for tasks like data compression, denoising and feature learning.

- Generative adversarial networks (GANs): GANs consist of two neural networks, a generator and a discriminator, which are trained simultaneously through a competitive process. The generator learns to generate synthetic data that is indistinguishable from real data, while the discriminator learns to distinguish between real and fake data. GANs are used for generating realistic images, video synthesis and other generative tasks.

- Transformer models: Transformers are a type of deep learning model based on self-attention mechanisms. They are particularly effective for natural language processing tasks such as machine translation, text generation and sentiment analysis. Transformer-based models like BERT (bidirectional encoder representations from transformers) and GPT (generative pre-trained transformer) have achieved state-of-the-art performance on various NLP benchmarks.

ML Model Evaluation Metrics

These are the most common evaluation metrics used across different types of machine learning models. We use examples from medicine here to highlight the power of AI for good in the world.

Performance Metrics:

- Accuracy: Accuracy measures the overall proportion of correct predictions, both true positives and true negatives, out of all the tests conducted. It's like calculating how often the test gets it right, whether it's predicting someone has a condition or not.

- Precision: In the case of Positive predictions, this focuses only on the tests that predicted a positive result, the person has a condition. Precision measures how often those positive predictions were actually correct, not just false alarms.

- Recall: This looks at all the people who actually have a condition and measures how many of those cases the test correctly identified as positive. It's important because a high recall means the test is good at finding true cases.

- F1 Score: This metric combines precision and recall to provide a single number that balances both aspects. A high F1 score means the test has good precision, avoids false alarms, and good recall i.e. catches most actual cases.

Other Evaluation Tools:

- ROC Curve and AUC: Using an example of ranking all the people tested from highest to lowest likelihood of having a condition. The ROC curve shows how well the test distinguishes between those who have a condition and those who don't. The AUC is a single number summarizing the overall performance of the ROC curve, representing the test's ability to discriminate between the two sets of people.

- Mean Squared Error (MSE), Root Mean Squared Error (RMSE), Mean Absolute Error (MAE): These metrics are used mainly for numerical predictions, like estimating the severity of a condition. They measure how close the test's predicted values are to the actual values. Lower values indicate better accuracy.

- R-squared (R2): This measures how much better the test predicts the presence or absence of a condition compared to simply guessing randomly. A higher R-squared means the test explains a larger proportion of the variation in the condition outcome.

Loss Functions – used during model training:

In the scenario where a medical test is being developed and refined. Loss functions are used to quantify how wrong the test is in its predictions. This feedback guides the improvement of the test's accuracy.

- Cross-Entropy Loss: This tests for condition presence/absence and tells how confident it should be in its predictions. If it's very unsure about an obvious case, this loss pushes it to be more certain.

- Hinge Loss: Similar to cross-entropy, but it's more forgiving if the test is a little uncertain about a case.

- Huber Loss: Like MSE, but it's less sensitive to extreme outliers or large errors in prediction.

- KL Divergence: This is more relevant for generating synthetic medical data like creating simulated patient records. It measures how different the generated data is from real patient data.

APPENDIX 3

Investment Framework for AI

STAGES	IDENTIFY	EXPERIMENT	LAUNCH	LEARN	SCALE
Focus Activities	• Define the AI strategy • Identify high-impact use cases for AI • Assign early resources • Form Investment thesis	• Run POCs • Model prototyping • Performance testing • Cost assessments • Planning for launch	• Deployment (pilot or full-scale) • User training • Integration with existing systems	• Performance monitoring • Feedback collection (users & KPIs) • Model refinement as needed	• Expand usage across the organization • Automate data collection & model updates
Input	• Outline business needs & opportunities • Available data sources • Funding • Tools	• Small-scale datasets • AI tools / frameworks • Technical & business KPIs • Data privacy assessment	• Production-ready AI models • Cost projections • Data privacy management	• Real-world usage & feedback • Sharp performance metrics • Dialogue with users	• Proven AI use cases • Robust MLOps processes • Promote buy-in across teams
Teams Involved	**Lead:** Business SME, Data Science & ML Leads **Support:** Data science & ML teams	**Lead:** Data Science & ML Teams **Support:** Business Unit SME, Software Teams	**Lead:** ML & DevOps **Support:** Data Science & ML Teams, Business Unit SME & End Users	**Lead:** Data Science & ML Teams **Support:** Business Units, ML and DevOps	**Lead:** Data science & ML teams, ML & DevOps **Support:** Business units, software Teams
Outcomes	• Prioritized list of potential projects • ML architecture • Spin up infrastructure	• Options on viable AI models • Cost-benefit analysis	• Viable AI models • Insights on performance • Cost-benefit analysis	• Model accuracy • Actions for further optimization • Rolling ROI assessment	• Wider business impact from AI • Metric driven decisions • Benefits realization

AI Investment Journey →

References

Books

Berkeley, Edmund C. 1949. *Giant Brains or Machines That Think?* New York: John Wiley & Sons.

Buchanan, Bruce G., and Edward Hance Shortliffe. 1984. *Rule-Based Expert Systems* Reading, MA: Addison-Wesley.

Minsky, Marvin, and Seymour Papert. 1969. *Perceptrons: An Introduction to Computational Geometry*. Cambridge, MA: The MIT Press.

Suleyman, Mustafa, and Michael Bhaskar. 2023. *The Coming Wave: Technology, Power, and the Twenty-First Century's Greatest Dilemma*. London: Penguin Press.

Journal Articles

Crabtree, Mark, and Amine Nehme. 2023. "What is Data Science? The Definitive Guide." Datacamp Blog. https://www.datacamp.com/blog/what-is-data-science-the-definitive-guide.

Crispin, Lisa, and Janet Gregory. 2009. "The Role of the Tester in an Agile World." In *Agile Testing: A Practical Guide for Testers and Agile Teams*, 32-63. Boston: Addison-Wesley. https://pdfs.semanticscholar.org/fd53/5070a5aa6b6d18bf57a4b84fbc1e8e0937ca.pdf

Felin, Teppo, and Matthias Holweg. 2024. "Theory Is All You Need: AI, Human Cognition, and Decision Making." SSRN. https://ssrn.com/abstract=4737265 or http://dx.doi.org/10.2139/ssrn.4737265

Hinton, Geoffrey E., Simon Osindero, and Yee Whye Teh. 2006. "A Fast Learning Algorithm for Deep Belief Nets." *Neural Computation* 18 (7): 1527–54. https://api.semanticscholar.org/CorpusID:2309950.

Kumar A, Boehm M, and Yang J. 2017. "Data Management in Machine Learning: Challenges, Techniques, and Systems." In *Proceedings of the 2017 ACM International Conference on Management of Data*, 1717–22. https://doi.org/10.1145/3035918.3054775.

Mijwil, Maad, Adam Esen, & Aysar Alsaadi. 2019. "Overview of Neural Networks." *ResearchGate*. https://www.researchgate.net/publication/332655457_Overview_of_Neural_Networks.

Rosenblatt, Frank. 1958. "The Perceptron: A Probabilistic Model for Information Storage and Organization in the Brain." *Psychological Review* 65 (6): 386-408. https://homepages.math.uic.edu/~lreyzin/papers/rosenblatt58.pdf

Rumelhart, David E., Geoffrey E. Hinton, and Ronald J. Williams. 1986. "Learning Representations by Back-Propagating Errors." *Nature* 323: 533-536. https://www.cs.toronto.edu/~bonner/courses/2016s/csc321/readings/Learning%20representations%20by%20back-propagating%20errors.pdf

Semaan, Peter. 2012. "Natural Language Generation: An Overview." *Journal of Computer Science & Research (JCSCR)* 5 (1): 50–57. http://www.lacsc.org/papers/PaperA6.pdf

Turing, Alan M. 1950. "Computing Machinery and Intelligence." *Mind* 59 (236): 433–460. https://doi.org/10.1093/mind/LIX.236.433.

Vaswani, Ashish, Noam Shazeer, Niki Parmar, Jakob Uszkoreit, Llion Jones, Aidan N. Gomez, Lukasz Kaiser, and Illia Polosukhin. 2017. "Attention Is All You Need." *Proceedings of the 31st International Conference on Neural Information Processing Systems* https://proceedings.neurips.cc/paper/2017/file/3f5ee243547dee91fbd053c1c4a845aa-Paper.pdf

Websites

AIMultiple. n.d. "How Do Neural Networks Work?" AIMultiple. https://research.aimultiple.com/how-neural-networks-work/.

Appenzeller g, Bornstein m, Casado m. 2023. "Who owns the generative AI platform?" A16Z. https://a16z.com/who-owns-the-generative-ai-platform/

Beebom. 2023. "How to Use Microsoft JARVIS (Hugging Face GPT) Right Now." Beebom. https://uaulis.asso.fr/?c=how-to-use-microsoft-jarvis-hugginggpt-right-now-beebom-bb-v6d0VBhz.

Datanami. 2022. "NVIDIA CEO Touts a Million X Speedup in AI." Datanami. https://www.datanami.com/this-just-in/nvidia-how-energy-efficient-computing-for-ai-is-propelling-innovation-and-savings-across-industries/.

Informatica. 2022. "10 Ways AI Improves Master Data Management." Informatica Blog. https://www.informatica.com/blogs/10-ways-ai-improves-master-data-management.html.

Insight Partners. 2023. "Generative AI from an Investor Perspective." Insight Partners. https://www.insightpartners.com/ideas/generative-ai-stack

International Organization for Standardization. 2022. "ISO/IEC/IEEE 42010:2022 Systems and software engineering — Architecture description ." ISO. https://www.iso.org/standard/74393.html.

Jain, Deepu. 2023. "Generative AI vs. Machine Learning: What's the Deal?" Medium. https://medium.com/@deepujain/generative-ai-2318965f0322.

Kaplan, Sarah E., and Andrew McAfee. 2019. "How AI is Improving Data Management." MIT Sloan Management Review. https://sloanreview.mit.edu/article/how-ai-is-improving-data-management/

Microsoft. 2023. "Artificial Intelligence (AI) Architecture." Azure Architecture Center. https://learn.microsoft.com/en-us/azure/ai-services/.

Newhauser, Mary. 2023. "Machine Learning and Generative AI: A Comprehensive Guide." Towards Data Science. https://towardsdatascience.com/what-is-generative-ai-a-comprehensive-guide-for-everyone-8614c0d5860c.

Nvidia. n.d. "What Is a Transformer Model?" Nvidia. https://blogs.nvidia.com/blog/what-is-a-transformer-model/.

OpenAI. n.d. "Language Models Can Explain Neurons in Language Models." OpenAI. https://openaipublic.blob.core.windows.net/neuron-explainer/paper/index.html.

Rose, Doug. n.d. "Machine Learning vs Generative AI: What's the Difference?" LinkedIn Learning. https://www.linkedin.com/learning/generative-ai-vs-traditional-ai.

Rutten, Peter. 2022. "Infrastructure for Artificial Intelligence (AI)." IDC. https://www.idc.com/getdoc.jsp?containerId=US49847222

Acknowledgments

Publishing a book has been a goal of mine for a long time. There are a few people I would like to thank for reading the early drafts and helping motivate me to get here: Columb Kane, John Crimmins, Ivan O'Dwyer, my editor Ellen Santasiero.

About the Author

Dave Muldoon brings twenty-five years of experience in the software industry to his exploration of the impact of artificial intelligence (AI) on modern software. Having worked as a software engineer, tester, solution architect and then as a technical, commercial and operational leader, he has a deep understanding of evolving technology trends. In 2015, he successfully sold a SaaS business he co-founded. Dave later played a key role in the acquisition of Immedis for over $500 million in 2023. He is currently working with an AI startup. His debut e-book aims to empower readers to proactively look at the challenges and opportunities that AI presents to everyone connected with software. Dave lives in Dublin, Ireland with his family.